ASK
SUZE

. . . ABOUT SOCIAL SECURITY

Riverhead Books
a member of
Penguin Putnam Inc.
New York
2000

ASK
SUZE

◆

...ABOUT SOCIAL
SECURITY

SUZE ORMAN

This publication is designed to provide accurate and authoritative information in regard to the subject matter covered. It is published with the understanding that the publisher and author are not engaged in rendering legal, accounting, or other professional service. If legal advice or other professional advice, including financial, is required, the services of a competent professional person should be sought.

RIVERHEAD BOOKS
a member of
Penguin Putnam Inc.
375 Hudson Street
New York, NY 10014

ISBN 1-57322-421-9
GEN-836

Printed in the United States of America
3   5   7   9   10   8   6   4   2

This book is printed on acid-free paper. ∞

Book design by Deborah Kerner and Claire Vaccaro

ACKNOWLEDGMENTS

I'd like to thank Allen Friedland, Deputy Public Affairs Officer of the Social Security Administration, for his invaluable expertise, and Peter J. Smith for his help in compiling this book.

ASK
SUZE

. . . ABOUT SOCIAL SECURITY

INTRODUCTION

Social Security. These two words may seem synonymous with the distant future. But with today turning into tomorrow more quickly than most of us are willing to believe, I strongly advise you to start learning as much about these two words as soon as you possibly can, no matter how old you are.

Why? For several reasons. The first is the most important: to protect yourself. Do you really believe that when you retire or become disabled or lose a loved one some eager representative from the federal government will be going out of his way to remind you that you are eligible for this or that set of benefits? In the final analysis, you and you alone are responsible for your money. I'm talking about not only your salary or the income from your investments but also the Social Security benefits—whether retirement, disability, survivors, or dependents—to which you are entitled in the future.

These days, some 30 million Americans receive Social Security checks, averaging $825 a month if they are age 62 and $953 a month if they are age 65. And this figure doesn't take into account the millions of widows and widowers who are receiving survivors benefits from spouses who have died, or the children of workers who are receiving dependents benefits.

It's not easy being old in this country. American culture is preoccupied with youth, and as a rule, we do not treat our elderly citizens with the honor and respect that they deserve. Job security has gone by the wayside, as employees who expected to be in the workplace for the long haul are routinely and abruptly laid off, to be replaced by men and women half their age. What does this mean? It means that more and more workers simply cannot afford to retire at age 62 or 65. Instead, they are obliged to keep working during the period when they expected to be enjoying themselves, thus turning their golden years into an extension of their earning years.

There is another very good reason for you to keep apprised about Social Security. In today's political climate, none of us can really be certain what form Social Security will take in our lifetime. Your guess is as good as mine. But chances are, Social Security will mean something completely different to you from what it has meant to your parents.

In short, keep your eye on what happens with Social Security. It may sound like a terribly abstract notion, but the decisions being made by politicians today will have an enormous effect on your future. Above all, you should try to understand the rules and regulations of the Social Security Administration, because, as I said, you and you alone are responsible for navigating the narrow byways of the Social Security system, and I want you to get what you deserve.

Read the following questions and answers, no matter how old you are. They will provide a basis for the sorts of questions that you should be asking as you confront the inevitability of tomorrow.

SOCIAL SECURITY: THE BASICS

Social Security is a general term used to describe a network of government programs designed to give workers and their families a regular monthly income after they have stopped working—whether because they have retired or have become disabled, or because they are the survivors or dependents of a worker who had these benefits coming to him or her.

Workers fund the Social Security system through regular deductions from their paychecks during their working years (Social Security tax). This money is held in trust and distributed by an agency of the federal government, the Social Security Administration (SSA). The amount of money an individual (and/or his or her family) receives is based on his or her past earnings. Workers become eligible for Social Security benefits when they have earned the requisite number of work credits based on their length of employment.

Do I have to have a Social Security number in order to work in the United States?

The Social Security Act does not require a person to have a Social Security number to live or work in the United States. However, all employers must pay Social Security taxes and make payroll deductions for their employees, and people who are self-employed must pay into the system as well if they make more than $400 a year, so in practical terms, you do need a Social Security number. If someone works without a Social Security number, he or she will not get proper credit for earnings, which will make him or her ineligible to collect Social Security benefits.

In addition, the Internal Revenue Service requires an individual to use a Social Security number on tax documents and to furnish this number to any person or institution (such as an employer or a bank) that is required to provide the IRS information about payments to the individual.

How can I make sure that I am going to get a Social Security number?

You have to apply for it. When you apply for Social Security, the SSA will give you a card that has your Social Security number on it.

When is the best time to register with the Social Security Administration and get a Social Security number?

The best time, truly, is at birth. For many of us, our parents registered us after we were born or when we were children. (If you don't know whether or not your have a Social Security number, call the Social Security Administration's toll-free number, (800) 772-1213, and give them all the information your parents would have provided when they registered you—such as your mother's and father's names, your date of birth, etc.—and the SSA will tell you if you are already registered.)

There's an incentive for parents to do this, too: to claim the child as a dependent on an income tax return. Any child you claim as a dependent on your income tax return must have a number, regardless of age. Getting a Social Security number is one of the very first things you can do to protect your child and secure for him or her the valuable benefits he or she may be eligible for in the future.

Children need Social Security numbers for reasons of their own, too. Your child needs a number in order to:

- open a bank account;
- buy savings bonds;
- obtain medical coverage;
- receive government or social services; and
- enlist in the military or enroll in college.

Am I allowed to receive two kinds of benefits, for example, retirement and disability, if I am eligible for both?
No. Many people find themselves eligible for two types of benefits, but you are not permitted to collect both, say, retirement *and* disability benefits. The good news, however, is that you will receive the higher primary insurance account of these two benefits.

What is a primary insurance account?
Primary insurance account (PIA) represents the amount of money a worker is eligible to receive if he or she claims their retirement benefits at his or her full retirement age. (Again, your retirement age depends on your year of birth.)

What is the average amount of monthly retirement benefits payments?
Currently, individuals receive approximately $825 in benefits monthly (or about $9,900 annually), and married couples receive approximately $1,300 in combined benefits monthly (or about $15,600 annually).

I think that Social Security is a ripoff compared to the private retirement plan that I have from my workplace. Can I drop out of Social Security?
No. Except for a very limited religious exemption, Social Security coverage is mandatory. But consider this: Unlike your

private retirement plan, Social Security provides disability and survivors coverage in addition to retirement benefits. Social Security also generally offers greater protection for dependents than private pensions do. However, it is true that most of us will have paid far more into the Social Security system than we will get back on an inflation-adjusted basis. In my opinion, the system is an archaic one, because it really is pay-as-you-go. By this I mean that when we pay into Social Security, our money is going to pay benefits for retired and disabled workers today, not for us years from now. Hopefully, someone will be there to pay for us when our time comes. But many people fear that this will not be the case, and that Social Security funds will have a negative balance by the year 2034.

Why is the prognosis for Social Security in the 21st century so grim?

Statistically, we are living longer and healthier lives. Furthermore, 76 million baby boomers will begin retiring in 2010; in about 30 years there will be nearly twice as many older Americans as there are today. At the same time, the number of workers paying into Social Security per beneficiary will drop from 3.3 to 2, straining our retirement system.

Many people think that their Social Security tax contributions are held in interest-bearing accounts earmarked for their personal future retirement needs. Social Security is actually an intergenerational compact—the Social Security taxes paid by today's workers and their employers, for the most part, are benefit payments for today's retirees.

Social Security is now taking in more taxes than is paid out in benefits, and the excess funds are credited to Social Security's trust funds. There is now about $850 billion in the trust funds, and they are projected to grow to more than $4 trillion in the next 20 years. Even so, benefit payments will begin to exceed taxes paid in 2014, and the trust funds will be exhausted in 2034. At that time, Social Security will be able to pay only about three-fourths of benefits owed—that is, if no changes are made to the current system. You see why this is such an important political issue—the security of future generations is at stake. The depletion of this system would be a terrible legacy to leave our children.

How do I know if I am eligible for Social Security?

The particular eligibility requirements for each benefits category—retirement, disability, dependents, and survivors—differ depending on the age of the worker and on the particular set of benefits you are applying for. But there is one hard and fast rule: to be eligible for benefits, you, or the worker upon whom you are drawing survivors or dependents benefits, must have earned a certain number of "work credits." You earn these credits over a period of years in which you have worked in what Social Security calls "covered employment."

SOCIAL SECURITY RECORDS

Does the Social Security Administration maintain a record of how much money I have earned over the course of my lifetime?

Yes. Incidentally, this is a very good reason not to cheat on your income tax return. Unless you declare all your income, it will not be recognized as such by the Social Security Administration.

What does the Social Security office do with my records?

From the records of your earnings, the Social Security Administration is able to calculate how much you should be paid for retirement benefits. (Disability, dependents, and survivors benefits are determined using different criteria.)

SOCIAL SECURITY CARDS

If I do not have a Social Security number and card, how do I get them and do they cost anything?
A Social Security number and card are free of charge. Call the SSA's toll-free number, (800) 772-1213, and ask for an application for a Social Security number and card to be sent to you. You can also pick up this application at your local Social Security office, or you can download it from the Social Security website at *www.ssa.gov.* All the information you provide on your application is kept strictly confidential and is not disclosed, except when required by law.

If you are registering a child, you can apply for a number in the hospital at the same time you furnish information for your baby's birth certificate. You will need to provide your Social Security number. The SSA will assign your baby a number and mail the Social Security card to you. If you apply for your child's number later at one of the SSA offices, you'll need to show evidence of your child's age, identity, and citizenship; show evidence of your own identity; and complete an application on which you must provide both parents' Social Security numbers.

What happens if I lose my Social Security card?
If you lose your Social Security card, call the SSA's toll-free number and ask for an application for a replacement. You will have to provide the SSA with documents that prove your

identity; these documents must be either originals or certified copies of originals.

Is it dangerous to carry your Social Security card in your wallet?

Keep your Social Security card in a safe place, rather than carrying it around with you in your wallet. If your card is stolen and you have evidence that someone is using your number for fraudulent purposes, call the SSA at their toll-free number.

For the record, it's against the law to use someone else's Social Security number; give false information when applying for a number; or alter or sell Social Security cards. Anyone convicted of these crimes is subject to stiff fines and/or imprisonment.

SOCIAL SECURITY
AND NONCITIZENS

Does a lawfully admitted alien need a Social Security number?

If you are a lawfully admitted alien with permission from the Immigration and Naturalization Service (INS) to work in the United States, you need a Social Security number. If you are a lawfully admitted alien who does not have permission to work, but you want to enlist in the U.S. military, federal law requires you to have a Social Security number. The number is used as your military service number.

State and local laws that conform with federal law may require you to give a Social Security number—even if you don't have permission to work. The Social Security Act permits state and local governments to use the number to administer laws related to taxes, general public assistance, driver licensing, and motor vehicle registration.

How do I get a Social Security number if I am not a U.S. citizen?

If you have permission to work, bring your INS documents with you to an SSA office when you apply for your number. If you don't have permission to work, you must call or visit one of the SSA offices to apply for a number. In either case, be prepared to provide original documents showing your age, identity, and alien status, and a letter, on letterhead stationery (no form letters or photocopies), from the government agency that is requiring you to get a number. The letter must specifically identify you as the applicant, cite the law requiring you to have a Social Security number, and indicate that you meet all the agency's requirements, except having the number.

If you are assigned a number for non-work purposes, you can't then use it to work. If you do, the SSA office may inform INS.

If I need a number for tax purposes but don't meet Social Security requirements, what can I do?

You can apply for an Individual Taxpayer Identification Number (ITIN) from the Internal Revenue Service. Visit the IRS in person, or call the toll-free number (800) TAXFORM (that is, (800) 829-3676) and request form W-7, Application for an Individual Taxpayer Identification Number.

SOCIAL SECURITY BENEFITS

What are the different kinds of benefits that Social Security gives?

RETIREMENT

Full retirement benefits have traditionally been payable at age 65 (with reduced benefits available as early as 62) to anyone with enough Social Security credits. The age at which full benefits are paid depends on the year in which you were born and will rise in future years. For example, if you were born in or before 1937, your full retirement age is considered by the SSA to be age 65. If you were born in 1960, then your retirement age is considered by the SSA to be 67. People who delay retirement beyond their official retirement age receive a special increase in their benefits when they do retire.

DISABILITY

Benefits are payable at any age to people who have enough Social Security credits *and* who have a severe physical or mental impairment that is expected to prevent them from working for "substantial" earnings for a year or more, or who have a condition that is expected to result in death. (Generally, earnings of $700 or more per month are considered substantial.) The disability program includes assistance to smooth the transition back into the workforce, including continuation of benefits and health-care coverage while a person attempts to work.

Dependents or Family Benefits

If you are eligible for retirement or disability benefits, other members of your family might be eligible to receive benefits, too. These include: your spouse if he or she is at least 62 years old, or under age 62 but caring for a child under age 16; and your children if they are unmarried and under age 18, under 19 but still in high school, or 18 or older but disabled. If you are divorced, your ex-spouse could be eligible for benefits on your record if you were married for 10 years or more.

Survivors

When you die, certain members of your family may be eligible for benefits if you earned enough Social Security credits while you were working. The family members include: a widow(er) age 60 or older, or age 50 or older if disabled, or any age if caring for a child under age 16; your children if they are unmarried and under age 18, under 19 but still in school, or 18 or older but disabled; and your parents if you were their primary means of support. A special one-time payment of $255 may be made to your spouse or minor children when you die. (Only children under 18 are eligible. If there is more than one child, the $255 will be divided among them.) If you are divorced, your ex-spouse could be eligible for a widow(er)'s benefit on your record.

Medicare

There are two parts to Medicare: hospital insurance (sometimes called "Part A") and medical insurance (sometimes called "Part B"). Generally, people over age 65 receiving Social Security qualify for Medicare. So do people who have been getting disability benefits for two years. Others must file an application. Part A is paid for by a portion of the Social Security tax of people still working. It helps pay for in-patient hospital care, skilled nursing care, and other services. Part B is paid for by monthly premiums of those who are enrolled. It helps pay for such items as doctor's fees, out-patient hospital visits, and other medical services and supplies.

SUPPLEMENTAL SECURITY INCOME (SSI) BENEFITS

The SSA makes monthly payments to people who have a low income and few assets. To qualify for SSI, you must be 65 or older or be disabled. (Children as well as adults qualify for SSI disability payments.) As its name implies, Supplemental Security Income "supplements" your income up to a certain level—which may vary depending on where you live. The federal government pays a basic rate, and some states add money to that amount. Check with your local Social Security office for the SSI rates in your state. Generally, people who get SSI also qualify for Medicaid, food stamps, and other forms of assistance.

SSI benefits are not paid from Social Security trust funds and are not based on past earnings. Instead, SSI benefits are financed by general tax revenues and assure a minimum monthly income for elderly and disabled persons.

COST-OF-LIVING INCREASE

Does the SSA adjust my benefits for cost-of-living increases?

Yes. The SSA automatically calculates an increase for inflation on January 1st of every year.

How does the SSA figure out how much this cost-of-living increase should be?

The SSA looks at the Consumer Price Index or CPI (see *Ask Suze . . . About Stocks and Bonds*), an index of prices for everyday goods and services, then adjusts the amount of your benefits accordingly. Since the cost of living rarely goes down, count on a yearly step-up in benefits of, say, 1 to 3 percent. SSI and Social Security recipients received a 2.4 percent cost-of-living adjustment (COLA) for 2000.

COVERED EMPLOYMENT

What is "covered employment"?

Covered employment refers to work for which you are paid monies from which Social Security taxes are deducted. For every year you work, and depending on the amount of money you earn during that year, the Social Security Administration will award you up to four work credits. When you decide to apply for Social Security, whether at age 62, 65, or 70 (or any age in between), the SSA will call up your work credits to see if you have met the eligibility requirements for benefits—i.e., whether you have achieved what the SSA calls insured status. The number of work credits that you need to apply for various Social Security programs varies if you are applying for, say, disability benefits as opposed to survivors benefits.

How do I know if my employment is considered covered or not?

Are Social Security taxes deducted from your paycheck? If so, then you, like approximately 95 percent of Americans, probably work in covered employment.

Seven years ago, I changed my name. Does this mean that my employment earnings since then won't count toward my Social Security benefits?

If your name has changed because you married or divorced, or for any other reason, go to your local Social Security office and fill out an application for a Social Security card. This application enables you to enter your new name legally with the SSA to ensure that your old and new names share a common Social Security number. You must be prepared to present documents that spell out both your prior and your present-day names, including, but not limited to, your marriage certificate or the request you made in your divorce papers to change or restore your name.

SELF-EMPLOYMENT

I'm self-employed. Does this mean that when I turn 62/65/70, I won't be eligible for Social Security benefits?

Until 1951, the self-employed were not eligible for Social Security benefits. Nowadays, self-employed workers pay taxes on a different IRS schedule. (If you are the sole proprietor of a business, you report your income and expenses on Schedule C, form 1040.) Don't worry, Social Security is looking out for you, too.

If I was self-employed before 1951, will my earnings in those years not count toward my work credits?

Unfortunately, that is exactly what this means.

If I'm now self-employed, will I pay more in Social Security taxes than I did when I worked for someone else?

Yes and no. Self-employed people must pay twice as much in Social Security taxes as employees pay. This is because no employer is paying a matching share for them. But there are special tax credits you can take when you file your tax return that are intended to lower your overall rate.

NONPROFIT EMPLOYMENT

I work for a nonprofit organization. Are my earnings considered covered employment?

As of 1984, your earnings are considered covered employment by the SSA. Before 1984, a great majority of nonprofit organizations exercised the option of remaining outside the Social Security network. This does not necessarily mean that because of the status of your workplace, you are now ineligible for retirement benefits. In some situations, employees of nonprofit organizations qualify for normal retirement benefits with fewer work credits than are typically required for most retirees.

This problem comes up most often with people who work for religious organizations. Typically, churches do not deduct Social Security tax from their employees' wages. In addition, these employees are often asked to dig into their wallets and pay the share of Social Security tax that an employer would normally be paying on their behalf, as if they were self-employed. Not only are the employees socked with a nearly 6 percent tariff on their wages, they must also pay annual income taxes! Employees of certain nonprofit organizations, including many religious groups, file a self-employment tax form with the IRS and pay this Social Security tax in full. Only then will their earnings be credited as "work units."

I am an employee of the federal government. Is this considered covered employment?

If you began working for the federal government after January 1, 1984, all your work since that time is covered by Social Security. Prior to 1984, your work was covered by the Civil Service Retirement System. We will discuss the rules that apply to federal government employees later in this book.

HOUSEHOLD HELP

My husband and I have hired a nanny to take care of our young children. Are we required to pay Social Security taxes for her? What can happen if we don't?

If you have hired any kind of worker—a nanny, a housekeeper, or a cook—and you pay him or her more than $1,100 a year for his or her services, then you are required by law to deduct Social Security and Medicare taxes and report the wages once a year. This includes reporting any cash you pay to cover the cost of the employee's transportation, meals, or lodging. Failure to report the wages on time may mean you'll have to pay a penalty in addition to overdue taxes. Please note: If the worker is under the age of 18, this rule does not apply.

Now, a reality check: Do most employers honor this law? No. Add to this the fact that many workers prefer to get their wages under the table every Friday afternoon so as to avoid paying taxes altogether, and you have a classic wink-and-nod mess. Unfortunately, a worker's desire to evade the IRS has consequences—of which he or she may not be aware—later on: The hours that the nanny or the housekeeper or the cook racks up are not included in the SSA's final totting-up of covered employment, and employees can lose out big time in terms of whatever benefits they should have coming to them.

As an employer of household help, how exactly do I report the wages I pay to the IRS?

You use your own federal income tax return (IRS 1040) to report wages over $1,100 that you paid to a household worker. As the employer, you pay your share of the Social Security and Medicare taxes, along with the taxes you withheld from the employee's wages, when you file your return.

In 2000, the Social Security tax rate for both employees and employers is 7.65 percent on wages up to $76,200. Of that rate, 6.2 percent goes toward Social Security benefits and 1.45 percent finances Medicare's hospital insurance program. If you pay your employee more than $76,200, you must deduct the Medicare hospital insurance portion of the tax, 1.45 percent, from the wages you pay the employee and pay the same rate yourself.

I work as a housekeeper for several families. How are my earnings and hours calculated for Social Security purposes?

Household work is credited somewhat differently from other work. A household worker will earn Social Security credit only for earnings of at least $1,100 from any employer. For example, if you work for three employers and are paid $700, $800, and $1,100 respectively (a total of $2,600), you would only receive one Social Security credit of $1,100 posted to your earnings record. The earnings from the other employers do not have to be reported and are not credited for Social Security because you were not paid wages of at least $1,100 by either of those employers. So if you can find such a position, it's better to work for a single employer in terms of earnings that qualify you for Social Security benefits.

For a long time, I worked as a baby-sitter for a couple who paid me my wages in cash. I assumed Social Security eligibility was irrelevant to me since I would be going back to my own country someday. But I was unexpectedly disabled, and now I need work credits to collect Social Security benefits. Is there anything I can do, or is it too late?

Even at this late stage of the game, you may be able to get credit for those unreported hours. You will need to provide the SSA with as much documentation as you can possibly pull together. Do you have any proof of employment? Have you kept a record of bank deposits from that time? If so, put these together, present them to your local SSA office, and hope for the best. But you should be aware that if the SSA credits your record with these unreported work hours, you may also have to pay your portion of the unreported Social Security tax.

WORK CREDITS

How do I earn work credits?

As I mentioned earlier, the vast majority of Americans work in a place of covered employment. That is, their employers deduct Social Security taxes from their paychecks. Again, an employee can earn up to but no more than four work credits per year, no matter how much money he or she makes. The rules concerning earning those credits have changed over the years. Before 1978, a worker was allowed to earn only one credit for each quarter of the calendar year in which he or she earned a certain amount of money. However, the SSA eventually realized that this restriction penalized many workers, in particular those who worked on commission and whose earnings could be high in one quarter of the year but fall short in another. So in 1978, the SSA altered the rules. Now it does not matter whether you earn a large amount of money during one quarter and less money during another quarter: You are still eligible for those four work credits a year.

Here's how you earn your work credits: For the year 2000, you receive one Social Security credit for each $780 of earnings, up to the maximum of four credits per year. In future years, the amount of earnings needed for a credit will rise as average earnings levels rise.

The credits you earn will remain on your Social Security record even if you change jobs or have a period of no earnings.

How many work credits do I need to be eligible for Social Security benefits?

The amount of credits you need to be eligible for Social Security benefits depends on your age and the type of benefit.

RETIREMENT BENEFITS

Those born in 1929 or later need 40 credits to be eligible for retirement benefits. People born before 1929 need fewer credits—basically one credit less for every year earlier than 1929. For example, if you were born in 1924, you would only need 35 work credits to qualify for retirement benefits.

If you work for a nonprofit organization that was covered by Social Security starting in 1984, a special provision applies that may allow you to receive retirement benefits with fewer credits. For more information, call Social Security to ask for a free copy of the fact sheet, "If You Work for a Nonprofit Organization" (Publication No. 05-10027).

DISABILITY BENEFITS

The number of credits required for disability benefits depends on your age and when you become disabled. If you become disabled before age 24, you generally need to have earned six credits during the three-year period ending when your disability begins. If you are 24 through 30, you generally need to have earned work credits for half of the period between age 21 and the time you become disabled. If you are disabled at age 31 or older, you need the number of credits shown in the following table. Also, you must have earned at least 20 of the credits in the 10 years immediately before you became disabled.

DISABLED AT AGE	CREDITS NEEDED
31–42	20
44	22
46	24
48	26
50	28
52	30
54	32
56	34
58	36
60	38
62 or older	40

SURVIVORS BENEFITS

The family of a deceased worker may be able to get survivors benefits, even if the deceased worker had fewer credits than are otherwise needed for retirement benefits. If you were born in 1929 or before, one credit is needed for each year after 1950, up to the year of death, in order for your family members to collect survivors benefits. If you were born in 1930 or later, one credit is needed for each year after age 21, up to the year of death.

Regardless of when you were born, your dependent children could get survivors benefits if you had six credits in the three years before your death. Their benefits could continue until they reach age 18 (or age 19 if they are attending a secondary school full time). Your widow or widower who is caring for your children who are under age 16 or disabled also may be able to receive benefits.

What if I'm nearing retirement age and I find that I'm a few work credits short?

Then you, like many older Americans, must continue to work past age 65 in order to become eligible to receive your benefits. You must somehow manage to accumulate those final few work credits, usually by sacrificing a couple of your retirement years to work, whether part- or full-time. Remember, the payoff is worth it, since once you become eligible for retirement benefits, you will receive them for the rest of your life.

THE AGE FACTOR

Is my age a factor in determining my Social Security benefits?

Yes. The amount of your benefit will vary depending on your age, with 1978 serving as an important cut-off date. If you turned 62 or suffered a disability before December 31, 1978, the SSA will calculate the dollar value of your past earnings from the day you began working. If you turned 62 or suffered a disability anytime after January 1, 1979, then the SSA's math gets more complicated. Any money that you earned before 1951 will be credited at its actual dollar amount (there is, however, an annual ceiling of $3,000). After 1951, there is a yearly limit placed on the credits you may receive from your earnings.

What does the SSA mean when they say retirement age?

As far as the SSA is concerned, "retirement" refers to the age when you first claim and begin collecting the full retirement benefits that you have coming to you.

Is age a factor as to when I can start to receive my full benefits?

Age most certainly is a factor. For people born before 1938, the normal Social Security eligibility age is 65. For those born in 1938, the full eligibility age will rise by two months for each year, until it reaches 66 for those born in 1943. It then stays at 66 for everyone born through the end of 1954. After that, the two-month-per-year climb in retirement age starts again, until it is finally capped at 67 for those born in 1960 or later. A chart on pages 34–35 will clarify this, and will also show you what happens if you choose to take early retirement benefits.

If my full retirement age is 65, do I have to be age 65 in order to start receiving retirement benefits?

No. For regular Social Security retirement benefits, you may opt to be paid beginning as early as age 62 (or three years before your full retirement age). But if you apply for Social Security at age 62, the amount of benefits that you receive from the SSA will be less than what you would have received if you had put off claiming your benefits until age 65. In almost all cases, if you start to receive Social Security payments at age 62 rather than waiting till you are 65, your check will be 20 to 30 percent less than you would have received if you had waited. Again, the exact percentage will depend on your year of birth. The rule of thumb with Social Security is that the longer you wait to claim your benefits, the greater the amount of benefits you will receive. However, in my opinion, you shouldn't wait. Get your Social Security benefits as soon as you can. I'll explain why later.

THE SOCIAL SECURITY STATEMENT

Is it possible to find out before I retire approximately how much my Social Security income, or my PIA amount, will be?

Yes. As of October 1, 1999, workers are automatically sent an estimate of their Social Security once a year, three months before their birthday. So workers born in June should get their statement in March. If your birthday has come and gone, and you have not received your statement of earnings, call the SSA at their toll-free number, (800) 772-1213, and request that your statement be sent to you. Or you can access the SSA website at *www.ssa.gov* and request your statement on line; you can even fill out the form on line.

What will the SSA form I will be getting tell me?
It will tell you:

1) How much you are estimated to receive at early retirement age (e.g., age 62), at full retirement age (e.g., age 65), or at late retirement (e.g., age 70).
2) If you have earned enough credits to qualify for monthly disability payments and what the amount of those benefits would be.
3) What your and your family's survivors benefits would be should your spouse die.
4) Your earnings history. Make sure you check this part of the statement closely, for these are the numbers the SSA is using to calculate your benefits.
5) The total amount you and your employer(s) have paid into Social Security and Medicare during your working life.

When you get the form, you will see that it is very easy to read. It is written in plain English—even its name has been changed from the Personal Earnings and Benefit Estimate Statement (PEBES) to the Social Security Statement.

How does the SSA compute how much money I will be getting once I retire?
The Social Security Administration calculates your benefits based in part on the average of your earnings since the day you

started working. (Remember, if you are self-employed, your earnings prior to 1951 are not counted.) Since you may be years away from retirement, the SSA also projects your future earnings; they assume that you will continue to earn what you currently are earning until the day you retire and they adjust your projected earnings for inflation. So keep in mind that the numbers on the statement will be conservative.

If I know what my future earnings are going to be, can I request that the SSA use the true numbers rather than projected figures in calculating my SS benefits?

Yes. You can ask the SSA for what is known as a customized statement. You give the SSA specific information, and they use this information to recalculate your Social Security benefits. Your next annual statement will reflect the information you provided to the SSA.

Can I order someone else's statement from the SSA, or can they order mine?

The SSA keeps personal information on millions of people. That information—such as your Social Security number, earnings record, age, and address—is personal and confidential. Generally, they will discuss this information only with you. They need your permission if you want someone else to help with your Social Security business, including making your statement available to someone else.

If you ask friends or family members to call the SSA on your behalf, you will need to be with them when they call so that the SSA representative can ask your permission to discuss your Social Security business with that designated person. If you send a friend or family member to their local office to conduct your Social Security business, they must show that they have your written consent to do so. Only with your written permission can the SSA discuss your personal information and provide them answers to your questions.

In the case of a minor child, the natural parent or legal guardian can act on the child's behalf in overseeing the child's Social Security affairs.

ERRORS: WHAT TO DO

How accurate is the Social Security earnings statement?
The accuracy of your statement depends on how old you are when you get it and the figures the SSA is using for your future income. If you are planning to claim retirement benefits at the age on the statement and if you are very near to that age, then your statement will be on the mark. If your retirement is far away and you don't know if or how much your salary will change as you grow older, your statement will be less accurate.

Should I be concerned about possible errors of information and/or calculation?
The SSA claims that during the Social Security Statement pilot program there was less than two-tenths of one percent error reported by recipients. Bear in mind that if you have changed your name for any reason during your lifetime, or if you have a hyphenated name, this increases the chance that errors may be introduced in your account. And employers may slip up and submit inaccurate information to the SSA, too.

What should I look for on my statement?
The very first thing you should do is make sure that the Social Security number at the top of your statement is correct. If it is off by even one digit, you could find yourself in a very messy

situation. You should also check that your average earnings as calculated by the SSA match your own earnings records.

What if I haven't kept any earnings records?

All is not lost. Most employers keep records of their employees' earnings on file, and you can easily arrange to get a copy. If for some reason an employer is unable to substantiate your past earnings, check to see whether you have on file any old bank statements or tax returns or deposit advises that might back up your claim. But be forewarned: The SSA is a slow-moving bureaucracy, and it can take a while to clear up an error.

I have contacted my old employer for evidence of my earnings, and I have all but one year's worth. Is there any hope for me?

Yes, there may be. The SSA has recently initiated a policy whereby a worker is allowed credit for earnings for a one-year period from 1977 to the present, even if he or she cannot show substantiated documentation for earnings in that year. This policy does have some limitations: It won't help you if the "missing year" was before 1977. Furthermore, the SSA has to have in its possession a statement of your earnings from the year before, as well as the year after, the year in question. Finally, the earnings that you are claiming but cannot verify must be consistent with the earnings from those two years. In short, if you tell the SSA that one year you earned $40,000, and two years later, you were still earning $40,000, but during the year in between, the one you cannot substantiate, you brought home $80,000, you won't have much luck.

APPLYING FOR RETIREMENT BENEFITS

How do I apply for retirement benefits?
When you want to begin receiving your Social Security benefits, you should proceed to the nearest Social Security office. Look in your phone book under U.S. Government, call the SSA's toll-free number, (800) 772-1213, or go to the SSA website at *www.ssa.gov* to find the location and phone number of the Social Security office nearest you. All Social Security offices make appointments with people who are claiming their retirement benefits. It can save you time to call ahead and schedule a time to go in. (Incidentally, the SSA mans its phone lines from 7 A.M. to 7 P.M. However, these lines are frequently busy, since the (800) number is a clearinghouse number for every conceivable kind of question people have about Social Security.)

At the Social Security office, you will discuss your case with a Social Security claims representative. Take note of this person's name! The SSA is an enormous bureaucracy, and it always pays to keep a record of whom you are dealing with, so that if any problems arise, you can contact that person directly.

Am I expected to bring any kind of documentation to this meeting?
Bring any and all papers that pertain to your retirement. You do not have to present your actual Social Security card, but you do have to know your Social Security number. You should bring your birth certificate or, failing that, a passport, or a driver's license, as evidence of your birthdate. If you served in the mil-

itary, you should bring in your military discharge papers so the SSA can confirm your dates of service. You should also bring in your most recent W-2 form, as well as banking information, since the easiest and most expedient way for the SSA to get your benefits to you is by direct deposit—wiring your monthly checks directly into your bank account. Remember, the SSA requires original documents, not copies.

What will happen during my consultation with the SSA representative?

You will undergo an informal interview. At the conclusion of this interview, the SSA representative will open a file on you. You will then fill out an application. Your SSA representative will look over whatever documentation you have brought with you and tell you if any additional papers are required.

When you apply for benefits, you will need the following information:

- your Social Security number;
- your birth certificate;
- your W-2 forms or self-employment tax return for the previous year;
- your military discharge papers if you served in the military;
- your spouse's birth certificate and Social Security number if he or she is applying for benefits;
- your children's birth certificates and Social Security numbers, if applying on behalf of your children;
- proof of U.S. citizenship or lawful alien status if you (or a spouse or a child) were not born in the United States; and
- the name of your bank and your account number so your benefits can be directly deposited into your account.

You will need to submit original documents or copies certified by the issuing office. The SSA will make photocopies and return your originals.

How long will it take for my application to be processed?
Processing your application can take from six weeks to two months. Your first benefit payment will reflect the date of your application.

I am going to turn 62 in eight months, at which point I intend to claim my benefits. When should I actually apply with the SSA?
If you are planning to receive your first retirement check on the first month in which you are eligible, you should file your claim three or four months before the birthday on which you become officially eligible.

If for some reason I forget or am unable to apply for my benefits, can I get credit for the months that I missed out on receiving payments for?
No. Retirement benefits are not retroactive. It is your responsibility to apply to receive the retirement benefits due to you.

I will be turning 62 on April 2 of this year, and that's when I plan to retire. Will my first benefit check be for the month of April or May?
Since you were born on the second day of the month, you will be eligible to receive benefits for the month in which you were born—April. In most cases, Social Security retirement benefits begin the month after an individual's birthday. To receive retirement benefits, you must be at least age 62 for the entire month. According to the law, an individual "attains" his or her age the day before his or her birthday. Since you were born on

April 2, you legally attain your age on April 1. Therefore, you are considered to be 62 years old for the entire month, and you are eligible for benefits in April.

My wife has long run her own catering business. She is turning 65 and wants to claim her retirement benefits. Are the rules regarding retirement different for someone who has run his or her own business?

In your wife's situation, the SSA will require additional documentation, mostly to make sure that she truly plans to stop working. It is an unfortunate fact that many people attempt to circumvent the Social Security system by saying that they are stopping working and arranging for a friend or a relative to be paid the salary they "would have been" making, all the while continuing to run the company from behind the scenes. Accordingly, the SSA is liable to be particularly focused on the infrastructure of your wife's business and whether it involves relatives or close friends. Your wife must be prepared to clarify what her exact relationship with her former business will be. If I were in your wife's shoes, I would request a meeting with a Social Security representative six or eight months before the time I intended to claim retirement benefits, to make sure that I had all the proper documentation in hand.

What if I apply for, and receive, retirement benefits, but then something happens that changes my particular situation?

A change of economic situation is very common, and you should know that you are not alone. You should also know that just because your situation has changed, whether it's because an irresistible job opportunity falls into your lap, or even if you decide all of a sudden that retirement is not for you, it does not mean that the SSA will suddenly lose faith in you.

Such things can and do happen. If you have applied for retirement benefits but you change your mind, the SSA will permit you to withdraw your application within two months of the date of your application's approval. If you find yourself in one of the situations described above, contact your local Social Security office and ask that your application for retirement benefits be withdrawn. Your representative will give you a formal document to sign that withdraws your application for benefits.

The only disadvantage of changing your mind? Any benefits that you have already received must be returned to the SSA. But you have to return only what the SSA has given you, not any interest.

CLAIMING YOUR BENEFITS

How does the Social Security Administration calculate how much my retirement benefits will be at the time I actually want to collect them?

The first factor the SSA takes into consideration is how much money you made on average over the course of your working life. The SSA calculates your benefits based on the amounts that you received in your 35 highest-paying years, and then, based on the year that you were born, it uses its own complicated formulas to come up with the final figure. But the rule of thumb is that if you earned an average of, let's say, $50,000 a year during your working years, then you will receive some 25 percent of that salary in benefits. If you earned $40,000, then you might earn 32 percent of those earnings. If you earned $30,000 during the highest-paying 35 years of your life, then your benefits will reflect a higher percentage of your average salary, perhaps 40 percent, and if you earned somewhere in the neighborhood of $20,000, then your retirement benefits could be as high as 50 percent of that amount. The SSA also takes into consideration your age when you decide to claim those benefits.

Can I choose when to begin claiming my retirement benefits?

Yes. You can start to claim your retirement benefits as early as age 62, all the way up to age 70, and at any age in between. There is a critical consideration to bear in mind: The sooner you claim your benefits—i.e., if you decide to claim them at the earliest possible time, age 62—the lower your retirement benefits will be for the rest of your life.

If I choose to claim my benefits at age 62, how much lower will my retirement benefits be?

That will depend on your year of birth. It used to be that we were able to claim full retirement benefits at 65 and early retirement at 62, with a 20 percent reduction in benefits. With the latest changes to Social Security, however, the answer is not so simple, and what you are entitled to under early retirement depends on when you were born. Consult the chart below to find out where you stand:

IF YOU WERE BORN IN	YOU WILL TURN 62 IN	THE BENEFITS AT 62	FULL RETIREMENT BENEFITS AT AGE
1937 or before	1999 or before	80	65
1938	2000	79⅙	65, 2 mo
1939	2001	78⅓	65, 4 mo
1940	2002	77½	65, 6 mo
1941	2003	76⅔	65, 8 mo
1942	2004	75⅚	65, 10 mo
1943–54	2005–2016	75	66
1955	2017	74⅙	66, 2 mo
1956	2018	73⅓	66, 4 mo

1957	2019	72½	66, 6 mo
1958	2020	71⅔	66, 8 mo
1959	2021	70⅚	66, 10 mo
1960 or later	2022–	70	67

Do you recommend starting to claim Social Security retirement benefits at age 62 or 65?

In my opinion, if you are not working and earning money, you should start to claim Social Security benefits at age 62.

Why do you think it's better take Social Security at age 62 if I'm not working even if I don't need the money?

Just do the math. Let's say at the age of 65 your full PIA amount is to be $1,000. At age 62, it would be 80 percent of that amount, or $800. If you started getting your $800 a month every month from age 62 to age 65, you would have received $28,800 in benefits. Now let's say that you did not need that money, and every month you simply put your benefit payment into a money market fund earning 4 percent. In three years, you would have a total of $30,517. If you then took that money and put it in a municipal bond at 5.5 percent, you average almost $140 a month. Add this to the $800 a month that you are getting in Social Security and you could be getting a total of $940 a month. That is only $60 less than if you waited till the age of 65 to collect your full $1,000. Remember, however, that that $30,517 is yours to pass on to your kids or to use in case of an emergency. And if interest rates were to go up, you might earn far more than 4 percent in a money market fund and 5.5 percent in a municipal bond.

Another thing to remember is that it will take you 12 years to make up for three years of not receiving benefits. At the age of 65 you would get only $200 more a month. At $200 more a month, how long does it take you to recapture that $28,800 that you actually got from the SSA? Twelve years. And if you had invested that $800 a month at 4 percent, it would take you 12.7 years. Finally, since we do not know what may happen to our Social Security system in the future, I would rather have my funds now than wait.

An acquaintance of mine said she ended up getting an interest-free loan from the Social Security Administration because she had to pay back her benefits because she went back to work. What was she talking about? Let's consider the following scenario: You are 62 and begin to collect Social Security benefits ($800 a month). A few months later, you decide to go back to work. You get a job that pays you $25,000 a year, which exceeds your annual earnings ceiling of $10,080 for the year 2000 as set by the SSA, thereby disqualifying yourself from receiving Social Security. You now have two options: The first is that Social Security will place you on "work suspense," where you will not receive benefits but do receive work credits. These work credits are then recomputed to determine your new Social Security payment when you stop working. The second is that you can simply withdraw your Social Security application within two months of its approval and repay everything they have paid you to date. No interest will be owed on this money when you pay it back. So you could have been collecting $800 a month, putting it in the bank, and earning interest on it. If you had gotten a job at 63 that disqualified you from receiving benefits, you could have paid back the money and kept the interest. Social Security effectively gave you an interest-free loan. By withdrawing your application, paying back the money, and reapplying at age 65, you will receive your full benefit, or $1,000 a month, which is more than you would receive if you had gone on "work suspense."

DELAYING RETIREMENT

What if I wait until I am age 72 to retire? Will my Social Security benefits be even higher?

No. The ceiling for benefit increases is age 70. So even if you continue working past the age of 70, you would still get the maximum amount of benefits that a 70-year-old person would get.

If I wait until age 70 to retire, does this mean that I have to put off applying for Medicare until age 70, too?

No. You can claim retirement benefits whenever you want, from age 62 to age 70, but you will automatically become eligible for Medicare benefits at age 65. You should sign up for Medicare benefits several months before you reach your 65th birthday.

What if I am forced to stop working earlier than I want to because of a physical ailment of some kind?

If you are younger than 62 and find yourself in this situation, it might be worth your while to consider applying for disability benefits as opposed to retirement benefits. There is no penalty for claiming disability benefits before age 65.

"NOTCH BABIES"

One of my friends, noting my age—I turned 80 last month—said that the SSA considers me a "notch baby." What is this?

If you were born between 1917 and 1921, the SSA considers you what they call a "notch baby." Because of your birth year, you are receiving slightly lower benefits than a worker with an equal earning record who was born before 1917. This situation came about in the 1970s, when the SSA realized that people born before 1917 were being paid too much money in retirement benefits. But the SSA was unwilling to play the bad guy and take away benefits from these retired workers, and ended up permitting people born before 1917 to hold on to their—slightly inflated—benefits. The SSA then proceeded to balance the benefits amounts for people born between 1917 and 1921. If you are a notch baby, you are not being cheated out of what is rightfully yours. Rather, people who were born before you are simply lucking out and receiving a little extra.

WORKING AFTER RETIREMENT

For financial reasons, I'm planning to work after I start to receive my Social Security benefits. Will I be penalized for continuing to work?

Possibly. Until you reach age 70, the SSA will deduct a certain amount of money from your retirement check if the income from your workplace exceeds a set amount for a particular calendar year. (By income, I am talking about earned income, which does not include the interest from whatever investments you have made. Nor does the SSA consider as earned income bonuses, deferred stock compensation, or income from retirement funds.) After age 70, you can earn as much money as you want per year without fear of being penalized by the SSA.

Is there a set amount that I am allowed to earn every year without the Social Security Administration penalizing me?

Unfortunately, I can't give you an absolute answer, since the amount changes every year. It also depends on how old you are. In 2000, for instance, if you are between the ages of 62 and 64, you are allowed to earn no more than $10,080 a year without being penalized by the SSA, and if you were between the ages of 65 and 69, you were permitted to earn no more than $17,000 without penalty. But if you are between the ages of 62 and 64, and you go over the annual limit permitted by the SSA, for every $2 that you earn, your retirement benefits will be cut by $1. If you are between 65 and 70 years old, the penalty falls to $1 for every $3 that you earn. And if you are 70 or older, you can earn any amount without incurring a penalty.

How do I report these post-retirement earnings?

Your earnings are reported on a conventional W2 form. The SSA will adjust its calculations using this figure.

Do I have to make quarterly estimated income payments?

In some cases, yes. If you are self-employed or if your income varies significantly from month to month—e.g., if you work on a commission basis—the SSA is within its rights to request earnings estimates from you. Typically, the SSA will send a beneficiary a form at the end of the year, requesting an approximate estimation of income. The SSA then uses this information to figure out the amount of benefits you should be receiving in the next few months. When the SSA receives your W2 form in April, it will make any necessary adjustments.

Again, if you are age 70 or older, these rules don't apply to you. After age 70, remember, you can earn as much money as you want without being penalized by the SSA.

For tax purposes, I need proof of what I receive from the Social Security Administration. What can I use?

Every year, the SSA sends all recipients of benefits an SSA-1099 form. This form shows how much money a given beneficiary has received during the past calendar year, and may be used as evidence of your accumulated benefits amount. People who receive their benefits checks via direct deposit receive a notice from the SSA when their benefits increase because of an annual cost of living adjustment (COLA). This COLA notice also serves as proof of earned benefits. If a beneficiary needs additional verification of current benefits, he or she can contact the SSA at their toll-free number. The SSA-1099 is also available on line at *www.ssa.gov.*

My next-door neighbor, who is retired, informed me that the income he receives from his part-time job at a local hardware store gives him an increase in his Social Security benefits. Is this possible?

People who return to work after they begin receiving Social Security retirement benefits may be able to receive a higher benefit based on those earnings. This is because the SSA automatically recomputes the benefit amount after the additional earnings are credited to the individual's earnings record.

The amount of income the SSA permits you to earn without a reduction in your Social Security retirement benefits varies every year, depending on how old you are. Most recently, in 2000 the ceiling on earned income for a person age 62 to 64 was $10,080, $17,000 if that person was age 65 to 69. Over age 70, however, there is no ceiling on the amount of income you can earn and still receive your full Social Security retirement benefits.

Will my retirement pension from my job reduce the amount of my Social Security benefit?

If your pension derives from work in which you also paid Social Security taxes, it will not affect your Social Security benefits. However, if your pension derives from work that is not covered by Social Security (i.e., federal, civil service, and some state or local government jobs), then this pension may reduce the amount of your benefits.

DIRECT DEPOSIT

Can I have the SSA put my Social Security check right into my bank account?

Yes. This is called a direct deposit. For getting money to its policyholders, the SSA prefers using direct deposit, a method whereby your benefits are deposited directly and electronically into your checking or savings account, whichever you prefer. If you wish your benefits to be deposited to you in this way, you must give the SSA the appropriate account and bank routing number.

What are the advantages of having my Social Security check deposited directly to my account?

Efficiency and security. No waiting period for your check to show up in the mail, no worry that your check has been lost or waylaid (or stolen). Some people, however, prefer to receive their checks in the mail, either because they do not have a checking or a savings account, or because they are changing banks.

If I sign up for direct deposit, how long will it take for my money to reach my account?

When you sign up for direct deposit, your first benefit check will be deposited in your account within 30 to 60 days. The SSA will notify you as to the probable date of deposit. Thereafter, your money is deposited and will be available to you on the morning of the actual day that you are scheduled to receive your benefit check. (Most people receive their benefit check on the third day of every month.)

If I sign up for direct deposit, do I have to stay with the same bank?

No. You can use the SSA's direct deposit method at any bank or credit union across the country. If you are changing your account, or account number, for any reason—you lost your checkbook or you have simply found a better deal at another bank—you should notify the SSA at once via their toll-free number.

SOCIAL SECURITY AND TAXES

Are my Social Security benefits considered taxable income?

Whether or not your Social Security benefits are taxable depends on your modified adjusted gross income (MAGI). To calculate your MAGI and whether or not you owe taxes, see what your adjusted gross income is on your tax return. Add to this figure all the interest that you may have received from any tax-exempt investments, such as municipal bonds. Then add 50 percent of your Social Security benefits. If the grand total, or your MAGI, is not above $25,000 or $32,000 for a couple filing jointly, then your Social Security benefits will not be taxed. If your MAGI exceeds $25,000 (or $32,000 for a couple filing jointly), compare the amount by which it exceeds the limit to 50 percent of your Social Security benefits. The lesser amount is the amount that will be subject to income tax. If you are married filing a separate return and you live with your spouse, then you may be taxed on your Social Security regardless of what your income is, for your Social Security benefits may be taxable from the very first dollar. Please consult with your tax adviser to make sure that the laws have not changed and that you are making the correct assumptions and calculations.

If my Social Security is taxable, how much of it will I have to pay taxes on?
Again, it depends on your MAGI. The higher your modified gross income is, the more of your Social Security you will probably pay taxes on. The maximum percentage you will pay taxes on is 85 percent of your Social Security benefits.

Can you illustrate this with an example?
Sure. Let's say you're retired, married, and enjoying an adjusted gross income of about $27,000 a year. Your combined Social Security benefits are $18,000 a year. The first thing to figure out is whether your Social Security is taxable. In order to do this, take half of your combined Social Security benefits ($9,000) and add this to your AGI of $27,000. This gives you a MAGI of $36,000. That's more than the $32,000 threshold amount that is allowed for taxation of Social Security, so you will have to pay taxes on part of your benefits. Next question is on what amount of your benefits will you have to pay taxes? To figure that out, we take your MAGI of $36,000 and subtract from that figure the $32,000 threshold amount for a couple. This

will give you $4,000. Now take 50 percent of that $4,000—$2,000—and compare that figure to what 50 percent of your total Social Security benefit is—$9,000. The law says the *lesser* of these amounts is subject to tax. Therefore, you owe taxes on $2,000.

If I am receiving dependents benefits or Social Security disability benefits do I have to pay taxes on them?
Possibly. All benefits paid out by the SSA fall under the above guidelines.

If my dependent children are receiving benefits, who pays the taxes—my children or me?
Great question: It's the children. At tax time, many parents treat their dependent children's benefits as if they were their own. So many parents pay taxes on their children's benefits under their own income stream, which in most cases is taxed at a lot higher rate than their children's income, when the children legally owe the taxes. Your benefits are reported under your Social Security number and the benefits for your kids will be reported under their Social Security numbers. Do not make the mistake of paying their taxes—at a higher rate.

MARRIAGE BENEFITS

I am a married woman who works and pays Social Security taxes. A friend of mine told me she'll be eligible for Social Security benefits based on her husband's work record, even though she's never worked or paid Social Security taxes. That doesn't seem fair to me. Does this mean that the Social Security taxes I'm pay-

ing are wasted, since I could get benefits on my husband's record without ever working?

Your friend is correct. However, the Social Security taxes you are paying are not wasted—not by a long shot. As a married woman who works and pays Social Security taxes, you are eligible for your own retirement benefits. You may get a higher benefit when you retire than you would if your benefit was based solely on your husband's earnings. You may be able to retire before your husband does and receive benefits based on your own earnings. Also, as a working woman, you are eligible to earn disability protection for yourself and your dependent children, and, in the event of your death, your survivors may be eligible for benefits based on your earnings.

Both my husband and I work and pay Social Security taxes. On which record will my benefit be based?

You will choose, based on which amount is higher. You are entitled to receive benefits based on your work record if you have worked long enough under Social Security—usually, 10 years, the minimum amount of time it takes to accumulate 40 credits—to become eligible. However, if the benefits you can receive as a spouse are higher than your own Social Security retirement benefits, you and your spouse will receive a combined benefit based on the higher spouse's benefit.

I am 58 years old and I have lived with the same partner for many years. Does Social Security make any allowances for partners who are living together but who are not married?

I'm afraid that the eligibility for many Social Security benefits is restricted to people who are married to each other. However, there are some benefits that accrue to people within a common-law marriage, which we'll discuss later in this book.

DIVORCE AND SOCIAL SECURITY

My husband and I are divorced, and I don't have a substantial work record of my own. Is it possible for me to claim Social Security based on his record?

You are eligible to receive dependents benefits if you and your spouse are 62 years of age or older, your marriage lasted for at least 10 years, and your marriage was dissolved at least two years ago (this refers to the actual date that your divorce became final). Please note, however, that this two-year waiting period does not apply if your ex-spouse was already receiving retirement benefits prior to your divorce. When your ex-spouse becomes eligible for retirement benefits at age 62, you can begin collecting dependents benefits.

What if my spouse and I have been separated for a long time? Can I collect dependents benefits?

Not according to the rules of the Social Security Administration. As far as the SSA is concerned, a marriage is a marriage until it is legally dissolved. If you live in Kansas and your spouse lives in Texas, and you haven't spoken for five years, but neither of you has gotten around to dissolving your marriage, then in the eyes of the SSA you are still legally married and therefore you are not eligible for your own benefits based on your spouse's work record. However, the clock has also still been ticking in regard to that 10-year requirement of having to have been married to your spouse. Bottom line, if you are close to the 10-year mark, wait until you have passed it to get a legal divorce so that you can qualify for Social Security on your spouse's record. But in order to collect, you must be divorced.

What if my former spouse decides to wait until age 65 to claim his retirement benefits? Does this mean that I have to wait, too?

No. Your former spouse must merely become *eligible* for his or her retirement benefits for you to begin collecting dependents benefits.

What percentage of my ex-husband's benefits will I get?

If there is only one of you receiving dependents benefits, then you will receive approximately 50 percent of your ex-husband's retirement or disability benefits if your ex-husband was born before 1937, and by varying amounts of between 20 percent and 30 percent if he was born after that. To make absolutely certain of what benefits you will be receiving, you should order a Social Security Statement.

Does the amount that I get in dependents benefits have any effect on the amount that my former spouse will be receiving in retirement benefits?

No. It is important to understand that by claiming these benefits, you are not in any way "punishing" your former spouse. Your dependents benefits will not take away from any of the money he or she will ultimately be collecting from SSA retirement benefits. You are simply getting what you are entitled to by law.

If I have been collecting dependents benefits on behalf of my retired former spouse, will these payments continue forever?

Your dependents benefits will continue for the duration of your lifetime, unless you remarry. This does not mean that you will not be eligible to receive dependents benefits based on the retirement situation of your new spouse.

What if I remarry and lose my dependents benefits, but my second marriage doesn't last? Can I reclaim those original dependents benefits?

Yes. And if your second marriage lasted for more than 10 years, too, then you could very possibly be eligible to claim dependents benefits based on your second husband's work record. You can choose the benefits of either husband as long as you did not marry a third time before the age of 60.

If my former spouse dies, will my dependents benefits continue?

Yes, though they will automatically become survivors benefits.

If my former spouse remarries, will this have any effect on my dependents benefits?

No.

Does the fact that I receive benefits take away from any benefits my former spouse's new wife might be able to claim?

No. Both you and your ex-spouse's current wife can be getting 50 percent (or whatever percentage) of the amount of your ex-spouse's benefits if you both qualify.

Does the SSA recognize dependents within a relationship where the two people are not married?

In general, no, though there are a couple of ways in which dependents benefits can be achieved in this situation. The first is that one of the two parties adopts the (age 18 or younger) child of the other one. The second way is if you and your partner live in a state that honors common-law marriages. As we have discussed at greater length in *Ask Suze . . . About Love and Money*, a common-law marriage is a relationship between a man and a woman (generally, same-sex relationships are not legally considered common-law marriages) in which the couple, for all intents and purposes, acts like man and wife and presents themselves to the world and to the community as a married couple. This means that they own property in common, share a bank account, and refer to each other as "husband" and "wife." The states that recognize common-law marriages are, in no particular order, Montana, Ohio, South Carolina, Kansas, Texas, Utah, Colorado, Alabama, Georgia, Idaho, Iowa, Oklahoma, Pennsylvania, and Rhode Island, as well as the District of Columbia.

DEPENDENTS BENEFITS

What are dependents benefits?
Introduced in 1939, dependents benefits deliver support to the spouse and to the minor children of a retired or disabled worker. The SSA's reasoning? That a retired or disabled worker with a family cannot live on the same benefit amounts as a retired or disabled person living alone, particularly when the retired or disabled worker was the family's primary breadwinner.

How does the SSA calculate dependents benefits?
The SSA calculates dependents benefits based on the number of family members and on the earnings record of the person on whom the family members are claiming dependency.

What are the actual amounts that a dependent can expect to receive?
If there is only one dependent, he or she will receive approximately 50 percent of the person's retirement or disability ben-

efits. If there is more than one dependent, the amount of dependents benefits are assembled into what the SSA refers to as a family benefit amount. The maximum family benefit amount can be anywhere from 150 percent to nearly 200 percent of benefits received by a retired worker, or 150 percent of the benefits received by a disabled worker. This does not mean 150 percent above and beyond what the retired or disabled worker receives every month. It means that after he takes control of the full amount of benefits to which he or she is entitled, the rest is divided among the dependents, whether they are a spouse and several children, or simply several children.

What if I am eligible for my own retirement benefits as well as dependents benefits?

Remember, the Social Security Administration has long decreed that a person who is eligible for more than one type of benefit cannot collect both. You may choose the greater of the two benefits to which you are entitled. Are the benefits you would receive as a dependent of a retired spouse higher than your own retirement benefits? Then by all means you should claim dependents benefits. What if you are 62, and your spouse is a few years shy of age 62? You should apply for your own retirement benefits, and when your spouse declares his own retirement benefits, then you can switch to dependents benefits.

Can I continue to work if I am receiving dependents benefits, or will the SSA penalize me?

Unfortunately, they will penalize you. The penalty will vary depending on your age. For every $2 of income that you bring in over the yearly SSA maximum of $10,080 a year, your benefits will be reduced by $1, if you are between the ages of 62 and 64. If you are a dependent who is between the ages of 65 and 69, the SSA will take away $1 for every $3 that you bring home in wages over the $17,000 annual ceiling.

What if I continue working past the age of 70?
Then there is no penalty whatsoever.

Are there any special rules for civil service or government employees who are earning a pension?
Yes. If you are earning a pension from a civil service or government job, and you also have claimed dependents benefits, the SSA has decreed that your dependents benefits will be reduced by two-thirds of the amount of your pension. This particular rule does not apply to pensions provided by private employers.

SURVIVORS BENEFITS

What are survivors benefits, and how do I know if I am eligible for them?
The Social Security Administration established survivors benefits for the spouses and children of workers following the death of those workers, regardless of whether the surviving spouse works outside the home or not. (Again, the worker in question must also have accumulated enough work credits during his lifetime. A spouse and children are eligible for survivors benefits only if the deceased husband or wife had enough work credits to satisfy the SSA minimum.)

The eligibility requirements are these:

You are a spouse 60 or more years old of the deceased worker.

You are a divorced spouse 60 or more years old of the deceased worker, and the marriage lasted at least 10 years.

You are a spouse who is under the age of 60, but who is caring for the child of the deceased worker, and that child is under the age of 16, or is disabled.

You are a spouse age 50 or more who has become disabled within seven years of the death of the deceased worker.

You are an unmarried child of the deceased worker under the age of 18, or, if you are still in high school, under the age of 19.

You are an unmarried, disabled child of any age of the deceased worker, whose disability took place before you reached the age of 22.

You are the parents age 62 or older of the deceased worker, and you were dependent on the worker's income for at least half of your total financial support.

You say that for me to be eligible for survivors benefits, my husband had to have accumulated sufficient work credits during his lifetime. How many should he have accumulated?

It depends on how old he was, and what year he died. If he was born in 1929 or later, and he died at age 30, he needs only six work credits for you to become eligible for survivors benefits. If he was born in 1929 or later, and he died at age 62, then he needed to have accumulated 40 work credits over that period of time for his spouse to become eligible for survivors benefits.

Are there any exceptions to this rule?

Absolutely! If your deceased spouse worked for at least one and a half years in covered employment in the three years prior to his death, you may still be eligible for survivors benefits.

How does the SSA calculate the amount of benefits to be paid to survivors?

Again, the SSA calculates the amount of survivors benefits based on the earnings record of the worker in question. The survivors are entitled to a portion of what the worker would have received in retirement benefits had he not died. Bear in mind, too, that the age at which you choose to claim survivors benefits will affect the amount of survivors benefits that you receive. For example, if your deceased spouse's full retirement age is 65, and if you claim survivors benefits at age 60, you will receive 71.5 percent of the full amount of the deceased worker's retirement benefits. If you claim survivors benefits at age 62, you will receive 82.9 percent of the full benefit amount. But if you wait until age 65, you will receive 100 percent of those retirement benefits.

When calculating the amount you will be receiving, you should know that if the deceased worker was making $35,000 or more a year, you will receive from $1,000 to $1,400 a month. If you have one dependent, this amount can increase to as much as $2,000 a month. If your spouse earned a middle-level income, say between $20,000 and $30,000 a year, your survivors benefits will be from $750 to $1,000 a month, and can go up to $1,600 if you have one dependent. If your spouse earned an income of $10,000 to $20,000 a year, then you will probably receive monthly benefits of $500 to $800, or up to approximately $1,200 if you are caring for one dependent.

Can I get an estimate of what my survivors benefit will be by ordering a Social Security Statement before my spouse dies, or is this too cold and calculating a thing to do?
Well, it's not a happy thing to do, but it is realistic. It is a very practical, if unsentimental, way to claim responsibility for your future. Your spouse's Social Security benefits represent some if not all of the money that you will be living on for the rest of

your life. And yes, you can order your Social Security Statement by calling the Social Security office, or again, by accessing the SSA website at *www.ssa.gov.*

I am eligible for both my own retirement benefits and survivors benefits based on my deceased wife's work record. If I claim survivors benefits first, will this have any effect on how much my retirement benefits will be?
No. In fact, it is a smart thing to do, since it allows your retirement benefits to reach their maximum potential. When you finally claim your retirement benefits at age 65, you should then choose the higher benefits package.

Can I do this the other way around? That is, claim my retirement benefits first and then switch over to survivors benefits?
Yes. Do it whichever way gives you the highest benefit last—the benefit you will collect for the rest of your life.

I've heard that the SSA offers a one-time-only survivors payment that helps defray the funeral costs of the deceased worker. Is this true?
Yes. If you were married to your spouse at the time of his or her death (not separated or divorced), then you are eligible to receive this one-time-only payment, which is currently $255.

Does this mean that if I am divorced I cannot collect this benefit?
If you are divorced and you have already qualified for survivors benefits, you are not eligible to collect this money. If a worker dies and is not survived by a spouse, whether divorced or still married, the benefits will be divided among the surviving children. Bear in mind, you must fill out an application to receive

this money within two years of the death of the worker in question.

What if I continue to work while I receive survivors benefits? What are the penalties, if any, assessed by the SSA?

It's a fact of life that even though many people receive survivors benefits, they still need to work full or part time in order to make ends meet. Just as with other benefits, the SSA will take away $1 for every $2 of earnings from a job that you bring in over the $10,080 yearly limit if you are between the ages of 60 and 64. If you are a survivor age 65 to 69, you will have $1 taken away for every $3 that you earn over the yearly limit. And if you are age 70 or older, you will not be penalized for earnings of any amount.

How long does a marriage have to last before a spouse is eligible for survivors benefits?

Technically, the marriage has to have taken place at least nine months before the death of the insured worker. But as with most SSA regulations, there are loopholes. For example, if you have parented or adopted a child with the deceased worker, the nine-month rule will be waived. The nine-month rule also does not apply if the worker's death occurred as the result of an accident as opposed to an illness, or if it took place while the deceased was serving on active duty in the military.

I was married to the same man twice. The first time, we were married for five years. The second time, we were married only two months before he died. Can I claim survivors benefits?

Yes. In the eyes of the SSA, you and your husband were married five years and two months.

I know that if I remarry, I will lose my survivors benefits. But will my children lose their benefits as well?

No. Even though your survivors benefits will terminate upon your remarriage, your children's benefits will continue as long as they live with you. Furthermore, if you remarry *after* age 60, you will *not* lose whatever survivors benefits you were receiving from your deceased husband's work record. And if you are age 62 or older, you may also be eligible for dependents benefits based on your new spouse's work history. In this case, you should choose the higher amount of benefits, survivors or dependents.

Our daughter, who had two young children, died two years ago. Her husband is planning to remarry, and his fiancée wants to adopt the children after the marriage. Will the children lose their survivors benefits?

No. The adoption of a child who is entitled to survivors benefits does not terminate the child's benefits.

My mother, who was a widow, died in late January. Social Security now tells me that I must return her January benefit (which was paid in February), even though my mother was alive for most of the month. Why is this?

Unfortunately, Social Security benefits are not prorated. To be eligible for a Social Security benefit check for a given month, the beneficiary must be alive the entire month. No benefit is payable for the month of death.

When a Social Security beneficiary dies, who notifies the Social Security Administration?

Many funeral directors voluntarily provide death information directly to the SSA. But family members of a deceased worker still have a legal responsibility to notify the SSA.

DISABILITY BENEFITS

How does the SSA define disability?

There are as many answers to that question as there are ailments that prevent workers from working. Long-term disability isn't just something that happens to the other guy. A prolonged physical or mental condition can affect men and women from all walks of life, and can strike anytime, with or without warning. If you are disabled for a long period of time, your savings can become swiftly depleted, particularly if you have to stop working suddenly, prematurely, and permanently. Living with a disability is never easy. But being disabled and lacking adequate income makes your situation all the more difficult.

This is where SSA's disability benefits come into play. While the average disability benefit in the United States (paid out, incidentally, to approximately 4.8 million workers across the country) is only $754 a month, this benefit can make a huge difference to a disabled worker.

Social Security benefits are generated by the U.S. government to people who qualify for payment under one or two programs designed to provide financial assistance to disabled workers. In order to qualify for disability benefits, a beneficiary (who has enough work credits) has to prove that he or she has a significant physical or mental condition which can be expected to result in death, or which has lasted, or can be expected to last, for a continuous period of 12 months or longer. This disability must prevent the beneficiary from engaging in any substantial gainful activity.

There is only one unbreakable rule as far as Social Security and disability benefits are concerned, and it is this: Whatever ailment you suffer, it must be defined and treated by the medical establishment. This means that you must have an official note from a doctor that your condition, whether it's heart disease, or chronic back pain, or severe depression, has been "validated" by the medical establishment, and that it is expected to last at least one year. The SSA will not accept this diagnosis from a chiropractor, an acupuncturist, or a physical therapist.

The SSA has compiled a list of conditions that it considers "disabling." Many people have combinations of the conditions listed below, and just because you may not have all the characteristics of one condition does not mean that you won't qualify for disability benefits.

The conditions named by the SSA are:

Heart disease of any kind, or chronic obstructive lung disease (emphysema), conditions which might result in the prolonged and persistent loss of heart or lung strength. Either of these conditions must be confirmed by a test such as an EKG or an X ray.

Acquired Immune Deficiency Syndrome (AIDS) and any related diseases, for example, pneumonia.

Chronic arthritis, which causes pain, inflammation, swelling, and limited movement and mobility.

Any type of brain disease that causes a diminution of judgment, memory, or intellect.

Cancer.

Loss of function in a limb.

Serious kidney disease of any kind.

Any diseases of the gastrointestinal system that result in severe physical diminishment.

Muteness.

Blindness.

Deafness, if it presents a seriously impaired ability to get along with other people, such that it prevents gainful employment.

There is a step-by-step, five-question process the SSA uses to determine disability. Here's how it proceeds:

1. Are you working?
If you are and your earnings average more than $700 per month, you generally are not considered disabled. If you are not working, or if you earn less than $700 per month, you are asked the next question.

2. Is your condition "severe"?
Your condition must interfere with basic work-related activities for your claim to be considered. If it is, you are asked the following:

3. Is your condition found in the list of disabling impairments?
If your condition is not found on the above list, the SSA must determine whether it is of equal severity to the listed impairments. If they determine it is, you will be found to be disabled. If it is not, you will be asked the next question.

4. Can you do the work you did previously?
If your condition is severe, but not at the same or equal severity as any of the listed impairments, then the SSA must determine if it interferes with your ability to do the work you did previously. If it does not, your claim will be denied. If it does, proceed to the next step.

5. Can you do any other type of work?
If you cannot do the work you did in the past, the SSA will seek to determine whether you are able to adjust to other work. Your medical condition, your age, education, past work

experience, and transferable skills will all be considered. If you cannot adjust to other kinds of work, your claim will be approved. If it is determined that you can perform other work, your claim will be denied.

You say that my condition, whatever it is, has to last a year or more. How can I possibly predict how long my disability will last?

Your disability must have lasted, or must be expected to last, at least a year. If for some reason, you recover before that, you are not in any way penalized, nor can the SSA demand the return of its money. If your case was approved by the SSA, then you are fully covered for disability benefits as long as you remain disabled.

Is mental illness covered under the terms of disability insurance?

Fortunately, our country is becoming much more enlightened about mental illness, though we still have a long way to go. The answer to this question is yes. Any condition that impairs behavior, interests, habits, and activities, or that impairs a worker's relationship with his or her colleagues, whether it's physical or psychological, is considered by the SSA to be a disability.

Are there any particular standards used by the Social Security Administration to evaluate a claim for Social Security disability benefits?

Yes. The SSA offers a free publication to physicians and other health professionals, entitled "Disability Evaluation Under Social Security." This publication provides extensive information about the disability evaluation process used by the issuing agency. If your doctor isn't sure how he or she should act according to SSA disability regulations, then you should make sure he or she gets his hands on a copy.

My personal physician has told me that I am suffering from a long-term disability that prevents me from performing any substantial activity. Am I automatically entitled to Social Security disability benefits?
Absolutely not. The Social Security Administration has its own statutory definition of disability, and no definition from any other source is automatically accepted by the SSA.

If I know that I have a disability, do I have to wait until the year is over to see a doctor and find out whether or not I qualify for disability benefits?
Absolutely not. You can apply anytime. In fact, you should apply for disability benefits as soon as you become disabled. (The typical wait for benefits is long enough.) Again, the important thing is to get a prognosis from a medical doctor that your disability is expected to last for a year or more.

My spouse recently suffered an injury to her leg. The doctors told her that after she gets her cast off and undergoes physical therapy, she will be expected to make a full recovery in 10 months' time. Even though this is less than a year, can she still apply for disability benefits?
No. Ten months is not a year.

Is it possible to be declared disabled by a commercial long-term disability insurance company and not by the Social Security Administration?
Yes. Each and every insurance company sets its own eligibility requirements based on its own definition and specifications of

disability. Therefore, it is very possible to be deemed disabled by a commercial insurance company and not by the Social Security Administration.

Is there anything else that I need to be aware of if I am going to apply for disability benefits?

Yes. One very important condition for receiving disability benefits is that you cannot engage in any gainful employment. The Social Security Administration defines gainful employment as any employment from which you are earning $700 or more per month.

If I keep my salary under $700 a month am I guaranteed to keep on getting disability benefits?

Not necessarily. The $700 figure is a general one. Bear in mind that the particulars of your situation—the condition of your disability, and the nature and quantity of work you find you are able to do despite your disability—will be assessed periodically by the SSA.

When the SSA is considering your application, it will assess whether you are able to do the sort of work you were doing before your disability. If the answer is no, the SSA next evaluates whether there is some other kind of work you could be doing in spite of your disability. For example, if your job requires a lot of physical activity, but because of your disability, you are no longer able to perform it, the SSA will suggest other, more sedentary kinds of work that you could potentially do.

How does the SSA figure out what I can and can't do?

In addition to the nature of your disability itself, the SSA considers a variety of factors, including your work experience, your education, and your age.

So it is the responsibility of the SSA to determine whether there is work that I can do, not my responsibility?

That is correct. The SSA has vocational departments that can help disabled workers find new kinds of work. They will also train you to use various tools and applications that can in many cases bypass your disability. In fact, sometimes the SSA requires a person who has applied for disability benefits to undergo vocational rehabilitation as a condition of eligibility for disability benefits.

Are Social Security beneficiaries generally encouraged to return to work?

Yes. In fact, on December 17, 1999, President Clinton signed into law the Ticket to Work and Work Incentives Improvement Act of 1999, under which disabled individuals are encouraged to go back to work.

I know that the Social Security Administration offers vocational rehabilitation and training assistance. But is it possible to receive this assistance and at the same time retain my Social Security disability benefits?

Yes. Check with the Social Security Administration for a complete list of rules that apply to training.

I have a job, but I need to modify my work space so that I can perform certain tasks. Where can I find help?

The Job Accommodation Network, or JAN, provides free consultation and services to disabled workers and employees who are interested in the advancement of people with disabilities. Their consultants understand the functional needs of the disabled and can provide a wide range of confidential assistance, though before contacting them, I would recommend discussing any major modifications, or changes, with your employer. The Job Accommodation Network can be reached at (800) 526-7234.

BLINDNESS

My wife has very poor vision. Is blindness considered a disability by the SSA?

Yes. If your wife's vision is 20/200 or worse *with* corrective lenses, according to SSA disability rules, she is considered to be blind. And she is eligible to receive disability benefits as a result of her condition if she has accumulated the required work benefits. If your wife is over age 55 and she can demonstrate that her blindness prevents her from being able to perform certain tasks that she was able to before her blindness, it will be much easier for her to collect disability benefits from the SSA.

Despite her blindness, my wife earns roughly $750 a month. Is she still eligible?

Yes. The earnings limit for people who are blind for the year 2000 is $1,170. This amount is subject to change. Your wife should definitely apply for disability benefits if her blindness in any way impairs her ability to work.

What if my wife, despite her blindness, starts earning more than $1,170 a month?

It depends on whether she earns that figure every month or brings home that amount only occasionally. If your wife earns that amount only occasionally, she can still qualify for disability benefits. But she should know that for the month that she earns more than $1,170, the SSA will withhold her disability check.

APPLYING FOR
DISABILITY BENEFITS

How do I apply for disability benefits?
Remember, your eligibility for disability depends on a verifiable medical condition and your inability to continue working as a direct result of that condition, whether it's physical or mental. Applying for disability is generally a much more complicated process than applying for retirement or survivors benefits, and typically it involves a great deal more documentation, including forms from doctors and hospitals. I advise you to be extremely patient, and to prepare yourself for a wait.

Should I request a Social Security Statement to find out if I have enough work credits before I apply for disability benefits?
Definitely.

Does it make a difference at what point during my disability I apply for benefits? Should I apply the moment I become disabled, or should I wait?
A worker must wait five months after he or she is disabled before he or she becomes eligible for disability benefits, i.e., before he or she begins receiving any disability benefits. However, the processing of a disability claim can take anywhere from two to six months. Thus, it is important that you not

wait until the five-month waiting period is up before you begin the application process for disability benefits.

What if I don't have all the documentation I need from my doctor? Should I apply now or wait until I have everything in hand?

Even if you don't have all the necessary documentation from your doctors, or any other medical service providers, in hand, you should still attempt to get this process underway as soon as possible. You can always provide the missing documentation while your application is being processed. The SSA understands that some documents are not immediately available, and will begin processing your claim if you promise to provide the documents at a later date.

So I don't have to wait until I have all the information I need before submitting my application for Social Security disability benefits?

That's correct. If you have sufficient information for the claims examiner to review your claim, go ahead and file your application. Attach a note to your application, informing the SSA exactly what information will be forthcoming.

If disability benefits are approved after the five-month waiting period, will benefits be paid to me retroactively?

While no benefits are payable during the five-month waiting period, benefits are retroactive to the sixth month of disability if your claims—including appeals—take a year or more to process.

What documents do I need when I am applying for disability?

Just as when applying for retirement benefits, you must provide your Social Security number, as well as the Social Security numbers of any family members who are eligible for dependents benefits. Bring your birth certificate, or if you don't have one, your passport or driver's license as proof of age. In addition, you should bring with you the names, addresses, and telephone numbers of the doctor(s), nurses, clinics, and hospitals that have kept any documentation of your particular case. You must also provide proof that a medical doctor has diagnosed that your condition will last for at least a year. While you are not required by law to bring in your medical records for your Social Security representative to look at, it will save a lot of time if you include them in your documentation. You should also bring a copy of your most recent W2 form, as well as a comprehensive record of where you have been employed over the past 15 years. Did you ever serve in active duty as a member of the U.S. military? If so, bring in your discharge papers, and make sure that they list your dates of service. Are you receiving any other kind of disability payouts, whether from an employer or a private insurance agency? Then you must also provide a record of these payments.

Where would I find the vital information I'd need to complete my application for disability benefits?

Review your tax filings for the past five years, or longer, if applicable. Look at check registers to identify any medical testing or treatment that you may have received. Ask your health insurance carrier if they can provide you with a complete record of any claims made on your behalf.

Do I need to produce my birth certificate in order to apply for disability benefits?

Yes. If you submit your original birth certificate, it will be returned to you after it is checked by the SSA. If you cannot locate your original birth certificate, then a certified copy will be accepted in its place. To obtain a certified copy of your birth certificate, contact the Board of Health, Office of Vital Statistics, in the city or state where you were born.

Is it my duty to obtain complete copies of all my records for the SSA when I am applying for disability benefits?
No. It is your duty only to list the names and addresses of all sources for records. The Social Security Administration requires that you authorize them to obtain copies of these records.

Am I responsible for any fees associated with the acquisition of records?
No. Any and all fees are paid by the SSA, since they are the ones actually requesting, and receiving, these records.

My wife is applying as a dependent to my disability insurance. What should she bring?
She should bring the aforementioned items, as well as documentation of the dates of any prior marriages, if applicable. This includes divorce papers. (The SSA wants to ensure that your spouse is married to you, and you only.)

What if because of my disability, I am physically unable to make my way to a Social Security office in person?
The SSA assumes that many disabled people will not be able to make a physical appearance in its offices. The SSA permits a spouse, relative, or friend to fill out the necessary applications for disability benefits. You can also arrange for a telephone interview or mail in your application.

What is possibly the most important question to be answered on an application for Social Security disability benefits?

The question regarding how your illness, your injuries, or your disability prevents you from working is probably the most crucial question you will have to answer. When you answer this question, you should provide as many details as possible.

After all the paperwork is filled out, what happens?

Your application is forwarded to the Disability Determination Service, or the DDS. The DDS will determine whether or not you are disabled in the SSA definition of this term, according to the information that it receives from your doctor, hospital, and/or other medical service providers.

What should I discuss with my doctor before I apply for disability benefits?

It's generally a good idea not only to discuss the reality of your physical condition with your physician before you apply for disability, but also to inform him or her of your decision to apply for disability benefits. This way, your physician will be better able to make the necessary notations that the Social Security office will be looking for—for example, to what extent you are physically limited or prevented from carrying out the everyday duties required by your work. Still, the DDS has its own team of experts on staff who will make determinations based on your medical records. Remember that despite the growing popularity of non-Western models of medicine, the experts at the DDS will not take into consideration the recommendations or clinical assessments of practitioners that are considered to be outside the realm of Western medicine. You must have a diagnosis from a medical doctor.

Does the DDS actually have doctors on staff?

Yes. And just because you have provided them with extensive documentation pertaining to your disability does not mean that they will not request even more! The DDS team will look at your records and decide, based on the kind of work you have done during your lifetime, whether your disability will prevent you from performing this work for more than a year. Then they will assess the severity of your disability and come to a decision as to whether or not, in their opinion, you could find any kind of work, not just the kind of work you have been performing over the past 15 years.

Is the DDS ever unable to come to a decision about the severity of a disability?

Yes. In this situation, the DDS will order tests or additional examinations. Please realize that the SSA, not you, is financially responsible for these tests, including any associated travel costs. These examinations serve to confirm certain points in your diagnosis on which the DDS is not entirely clear. For example, are your motor abilities affected to the extent that you cannot work?

Will I be meeting with a whole new team of doctors who are unfamiliar with my case?

Probably not. The DDS often calls on the doctor who first provided your diagnosis. However, if that doctor does not specialize in the disability you are claiming and you have not yet been seen by a specialist in this particular field, the DDS will probably send you to a doctor who is not familiar with your case.

Can I refuse additional tests?

Of course you can, but if you do, you will no longer be eligible to receive disability benefits. I would strongly advise going along with them.

Should I keep a copy of my completed Social Security disability application in my files?

Yes. Whenever you release any intimate and/or important information about yourself, you should keep a copy of the paperwork. You might need this information to review your claim if for some reason an appeal of denied benefits becomes necessary. It's also always wise to have proof of filing. If you file by mail, send your application for Social Security disability by certified mail, return receipt requested.

How soon after filing an application for disability benefits can I expect to hear from the Social Security Administration?

A receipt for your claim for Social Security disability benefits will be sent to you soon after the claim is received by the Social Security Administration. The receipt will indicate when you should expect to hear from the agency again. Here's a tip: If you are obligated to apply for Social Security disability benefits as a term of other disability benefits, you should duplicate your receipt and forward a copy to the appropriate party. Don't forget to keep proof of this mailing, too.

What happens when I next hear from the SSA?

You will receive a notice of decision from the SSA. Your notice of decision will contain notice of a favorable or unfavorable determination of eligibility for benefits, as well as various instructions for further action, should any further action be required of you by the SSA. If so, you should pay careful attention to any time restrictions stated in the notice of decision. This way, you will avoid any possible loss of benefits due to a failure to properly comply with filing rules.

DISABILITY BENEFIT PAYMENTS

Where can I find a complete list of my responsibilities as a Social Security disability insurance recipient?
Everything you need to know is contained in a free publication entitled "What You Need to Know When You Get Disability Benefits." You can order this booklet by calling the SSA's toll-free number, (800) 772-1213, or by accessing the SSA's website at *www.ssa.gov*.

How does the SSA determine how much money I will be paid in disability benefits?
By using actuarial tables. The amount that you or your family will receive is based on the average income you have earned over the years. If you know that someday your condition will render you unable to continue working at the job you currently hold, it is possible to learn beforehand the approximate amount of your disability benefits. A worker who has earned an average income of $30,000 or more during his lifetime is eligible to receive disability payments averaging from $12,000 to $15,360 a year. If the worker earned from $20,000 to $30,000 during his lifetime, then he is eligible to receive payments averaging from $8,400 to $12,000 annually. If he earned from $10,000 to $20,000, he is eligible to receive disability benefits anywhere from $6,000 to $9,000 a year.

Does the SSA figure in cost-of-living increases with disability payments, as they do with retirement benefits?
Yes, and again this small annual increase for inflation (typically

anywhere from 1 to 3 percent) is tied to the Consumer Price Index.

Can a person survive solely on disability benefits?

It can be extremely difficult, if not impossible, to survive on the amount of money that the SSA provides in its disability benefits. For that reason and others, it is important that you find out whether there is any job that your limited physical condition will permit you to do. It is also important that you find out exactly what benefits you may have coming to you from any other sources. Remember, the Social Security Administration with all its attendant benefits, whether retirement, disability, survivors, or dependents, was initiated in the 1930s as a kind of padding, not as a replacement for your entire income.

Won't my benefits be lowered by the SSA if I find some other kind of work that I can do?

Not necessarily. However, bear in mind that if you consistently earn enough money that your work is considered "substantial gainful employment," then it is possible that the SSA might not consider you disabled any longer, and they could cut off your payments. Remember, the SSA usually permits you to earn up to $700 (or $1,170 if you are legally blind) a month before it begins to question whether the work you are doing is "gainful." The SSA reasons, sensibly, that if you are able to make this kind of money, there's no reason for you to be on disability in the first place. Also, please note that the SSA is an organization highly experienced in all kinds of attempts by citizens to evade its various review processes. Some people arrange for friends or family to receive the money that they themselves are making. Please do not compromise your benefits in this way, because if the SSA discovers that you are attempting to cheat the system, your benefits can and will be cut off very suddenly. You might also become the target of a fraud investigation by the SSA's Office of Investigations.

THE REVIEW PROCESS

I thought disability benefits were permanent! Do you mean to say that the SSA comes in and does a check every now and then to see how I'm doing?
That's exactly what I am saying. Disability benefits are not necessarily for the duration of your life. How long you receive them depends on the kind of disability you have. Do you have a condition that your doctor expects to improve over time? Is there a good chance that you will be back on your feet within two or three years? If so, the SSA can come in later, review your condition again, and decide whether or not you are able to go back to work.

How often will the SSA check on my condition?
If your doctor fully anticipates that your condition, whatever it is, will improve over time, then your case will be subject to review anywhere from six months to a year and a half following your initial approval for disability benefits.

What if my condition is not expected to improve?
Even if your condition is not expected to improve, the SSA will still keep tabs on you. In this situation, the SSA will review your case approximately every five to seven years.

What does the actual review process entail?
Typically, you will receive in the mail a letter from Social Security, requesting a sit-down interview at your local SSA office.

There, you will be asked about your medical condition, as well as about any supplementary work you are doing.

How should I prepare for this meeting?

Bring with you any documentation associated with your disability, and, if applicable, your current employment. This includes the name, address, and phone number of your doctor, the hospital at which you are being treated, your place of work, the amount of your present-day income, and the name of a contact person the SSA should get in touch with to verify that all the information you have submitted is accurate.

Then what happens?

After this preliminary interview, the Social Security representative worker will forward your case file to the DDS. After reviewing the information you provided, the DDS will contact your doctor, hospital, or other medical provider in order to confirm the particulars of your condition. In some cases, the DDS may order you to undergo another physical exam relating to your disability. Based on the results of this exam and the amount of income that you are receiving from employment, if applicable, the DDS will make a ruling about your case. In this situation, the DDS is looking to see whether your disability has improved since the last time you checked in with the agency, and whether you are earning sufficient income for you to be considered gainfully employed. If the DDS finds no evidence of either of these factors, then your disability benefits will continue as before.

What if the DDS decides to cut me off?

You have a right to appeal their decision. And bear in mind that if the DDS rules that you are no longer eligible to receive disability benefits, you have up to three months to continue receiving these benefits while you look for a new job.

TRIAL WORK PERIODS

What if I attempt to go back to work, but my condition recurs or I develop some other disability that makes me realize that I made the wrong decision?

Don't worry. This is a common occurrence, and the SSA has long made allowances for it. The SSA permits a disabled worker to return to work for nine months or less while still receiving full disability benefits during a particular five-year period. This is what is known as a trial work period. Incidentally, the nine months do not have to be spent at only one job. Often, a worker returns to work and finds that he or she is unable to perform the tasks required by that particular job, so he or she tries another job and finds that one more to his liking or more suited to his diminished abilities. You may try a job for a couple of months, find that it is not right for you, then reapply for the same job eight months or two years later, and this time around, find that a change in your condition makes it easier for you to perform the work. As long as these attempts fall within a five-year period, they are all right with the SSA.

What happens when my nine-month trial work period expires?

At this point, the DDS reassesses your ability to work. If you have not brought in an average income of $700 a month or more (remember, if you are legally blind, you can bring in $1,170 a month), the SSA will simply give you the go-ahead to continue your disability benefits.

Even though I earn good money from my job, a great chunk of my salary goes toward expenses relating to my disability!

The SSA will take these expenses into consideration when it considers your particular case and how much income you are earning. It is crucial, however, that you hold on to any records of money that you paid out for health-related expenses, such as receipts or canceled checks.

What if I'm able to return completely to work? Will my disability benefits completely disappear?

First of all, congratulations on your return to work! Love and work are the two most important aspects of our lives, and most people, if given the chance, would choose working over not working. The SSA will continue to keep tabs on you for three years following your reinstatement at the workplace. If there is a month in which you do not earn $700, you will receive your disability benefits for that month. (If you find yourself in this situation, you do not have to reapply for disability. Simply report this earnings information to your disability representative.)

What about any Medicare coverage to which I was entitled because of my disability? Will this stop when I go back to work?

Medicare coverage continues for three years and three months following the conclusion of your trial work period. Effective October 1, 2000, you may maintain your Medicare coverage for an additional four and a half years after that three-year, three-month period is over by paying monthly premiums.

What if after a year at my job I find that I am unable to keep working because of my old disability?

The SSA makes allowances for such situations. Let's say that you return to work and stop receiving disability benefits. But within 15 months of completing your nine-month trial work period you find yourself again unable to work, whether because of the recurrent disability or a new one. You should contact your Social Security disability worker. Again, in this situation, you will not have to reapply for benefits.

DISABILITY AND MEDICARE

My husband returned to work and then suffered an accident. This disability is different from his original disability. Does he have to reapply for disability benefits?
No. He does not have to go through the application process again. His new period of disability payments will begin the first month of his new disability. The same is true for his Medicare benefits, if they were in place during your husband's initial disability. They will take effect at the same time the new disability payments take effect.

My husband was not eligible for Medicare during his first disability! How long must he be on disability before he is allowed to apply for Medicare?
Twenty-four months, or two years. Incidentally, those 24 months do not necessarily have to be consecutive. This is true even if your husband has not reached the standard qualifying age of 65.

The length of time that your husband was previously receiving disability payments will be added to the new period of his receiving disability payments until he has reached the qualifying number of 24 months. Then he is eligible to receive full Medicare coverage.

If I'm receiving disability benefits from the SSA, am I permitted to receive other disability payments, i.e., from an employer or from the Veterans Administration? Or do I have to give those up?

The SSA permits workers to receive disability coverage from other sources.

Can I collect workers compensation at the same time I am receiving disability benefits?

Yes, the SSA permits this as well, though with an important restriction: The total of your disability payments and the amount of workers comp you are receiving cannot be more than 80 percent of your average paycheck prior to your disability. If the total is greater than 80 percent, the SSA will reduce your disability benefits until the total reflects that 80 percent figure.

Because of my disability, I am unable to perform certain functions, including opening my mail, endorsing checks, and going to the bank. Can I legally entrust these duties to someone else?

Yes. You can arrange this informally with a friend or a family member, or you can go so far as to have this person's name added to your Social Security documentation. This latter option might be safer in the long run, because everything is then legal, and Social Security has in writing appointed that person to be your substitute payee. If you are considering this latter option, the person you have chosen as your substitute payee must provide medical evidence that you are unable to handle these particular chores by yourself. The payee must sign a legal affidavit that he or she is managing your SSA payment on your behalf. And the payee must also keep careful records that demonstrate to the SSA that the monthly benefit check has been used to take care of the beneficiary.

Denied Benefits: The Basics

What happens if I have applied for a Social Security benefit that I believe I am entitled to, and for some reason, the SSA turns me down? Do I have any recourse?
Being turned down by the SSA is very common, particularly, as you might imagine, in the case of disability, since you and the SSA might disagree strongly as to the severity of your condition or whether it prevents you from carrying out your normal work duties. You may appeal any decision that the SSA has made regarding your application, whether you are turned down summarily for benefits, or the amount that you receive is less than you had anticipated, or the SSA has decided to terminate one set of benefits. The appeal process is different for each kind of benefits. But there are certain general rules regarding the appeal process, and we will go over them in order.

What is the first step in the appeal process?
The first thing you should do, regardless of the sort of benefit you intend to appeal, is ask for a reconsideration of your application, officially known as a request for reconsideration. You can either pick up a copy of the request for reconsideration form at your local Social Security office, or you can call the SSA's toll-free number, and they will send you one, or you can download it from the SSA website.

What kind of information will I have to provide on this form?
You will be asked to provide basic information, such as your name, your address, your Social Security number, and what

kind of benefits you originally applied for. You also will be asked to state in a few sentences why you wish to appeal the SSA's decision. You should state your case as briefly as possible. For example, if you are disabled and you do not think the SSA had a full accounting of your situation, you should write something to the effect of, "The SSA did not take into consideration the fact that because of my paralysis, or poor eyesight, etc., I cannot do X, Y, and Z. Enclosed please find a letter from my doctor that spells out my limitations."

As with any important financial document, keep a copy for your records.

Will my benefits continue while I'm appealing a decision made by the SSA?

It depends on the nature of your appeal. If you are appealing a disability decision, your monthly disability benefits will typically continue. For example, if you have been receiving disability benefits, and the SSA decides that your condition has improved and you are no longer eligible for these payments, you are still legally able to receive those benefits during an appeal process. (Incidentally, the same is true if you are receiving SSI benefits, and the SSA decides that your assets or income have reached such a level that you are no longer eligible for these payments.) But pay very close attention to the next question.

What happens if my appeal is turned down? Will I have to reimburse the SSA for the benefits that they continued to send me while my appeal was being considered?

In many cases, yes, you will. You will not, however, have to pay the SSA any interest on this money.

How long do I have to appeal a decision that I disagree with?

You have up to 60 days from the date you are first informed by the SSA of their decision to notify the agency in writing that you intend to appeal that decision.

Is an appeal worth it? Or will it blacken my name forever in the offices of the SSA?

An appeal is actually a very simple, commonplace procedure, and no, it will not blacken your name. Remember, this is your life and your money we are talking about, and it's always worth taking those extra steps to ensure the best possible future for yourself. It is also a plain fact that many decisions made by the SSA are reversed on appeal. Incidentally, an appeal need not be a long-drawn-out or overly complicated process. Often, it simply involves restating the case you made the first time you applied for disability benefits. Sometimes, you will simply be providing a few additional pieces of material or documentation as evidence to bolster your case. (This is particularly true when you are appealing a decision regarding a disability.)

After I submit my request for reconsideration, am I required to make an appearance at the Social Security office?

No. Appeals are generally handled via the postal service and the telephone.

How long does the appeal process take?

After your application has been received, you will receive written notice from the SSA, usually within 30 days. If you are appealing a dispute over disability, these decisions can often take several months, especially if the SSA has to consider new evidence supplied by a physician.

APPEALING DISABILITY CLAIMS

I have been receiving disability benefits for the past three years, but two months ago, the SSA decided that my condition no longer merits disability payments. How can I appeal this decision?

After filing the requisite request for reconsideration, you have the right to meet with a Social Security representative in person to go over your case. As ever, the meeting is squarely in your hands. You must request what is known as a disability hearing. You may do this either on the request for reconsideration form, or you may inform your representative that you wish to schedule a disability hearing.

Recently the SSI notified me that they are going to discontinue my benefits. What do I do?

What you do depends in large part on the particulars of your situation. If, for example, you have been turned down for SSI benefits because the SSI office considers your assets and income to be over the maximum allowable ceiling, you should request a meeting with the person who was responsible for handling your claim. Bring whatever evidence you deem necessary to bolster your argument. If you have been receiving SSI benefits for a while, and the SSI office determines for whatever reason that you are no longer eligible for these benefits, or the SSI office has decided to reduce the amount that you receive every month, then you can request what is known as a formal conference.

What happens during a formal conference?

A formal conference (which is actually misnamed, as it is not formal in the least) is a meeting during which you are allowed to present whatever materials or documentation necessary to enhance your application. This is a just-the-facts sort of hearing. The representative in charge does not want to hear the story of your life or be presented with a recapitulation of the paperwork he or she already has on file. Instead, the meeting will focus on the specific reason that the SSA office reduced or eliminated your benefits.

What happens if my appeal is unsuccessful? Can I appeal a second time?

Yes. If you are still willing to pursue your claim, now is the time for you to request a formal administrative hearing. You have 60 days from the time the SSA notifies you that your appeal was unsuccessful to apply for a request for this hearing. There is another form to fill out, known as the request for hearing by administrative law judge form. It is available either at your local Social Security office, or by calling the SSA's toll-free number at (800) 772-1213, or on line at the SSA website. After you fill out and send in this request, the SSA will notify you as to the time and the place of your hearing.

What happens during this hearing?

The formal administrative hearing is held before an administrative law judge who, while connected with the SSA, has never considered your case before, so the material he bases his determination upon is new to him. During this hearing—which, by the way, is recorded—you will have the opportunity to present whatever evidence you see fit to bolster your claim. You may also arrange for witnesses to testify on your behalf. This may sound like a Perry Mason–type courtroom trial, but the reality is far less stringent than that. The judge may ask you questions about your case, but don't worry, there is no cross-examination!

Should my attorney be present?

I would certainly advise having a lawyer or some kind of representative by your side at the hearing. Before the hearing, I would also strongly advise that you become as fully conversant with your Social Security file as possible, since you want to arrive as fully prepared as you can be. You can get access to your file by calling your local SSA office. When you look at your file, you want to make sure there are no mistakes, and that all the documentation that is supposed to be in your file is indeed there. You should also have in hand as many pieces of documentation—medical, legal—as are relevant to your case.

Will the judge reach a decision right then and there?

No. The judge will issue a decision in writing anywhere from a month to two months from the date of the hearing.

If the administrative law judge turns down my second appeal, is that it? Or can I appeal a third time?

You can appeal again, though this time around, your chances of the SSA's reversing its decision are fairly slim. As before, you have 60 days from the date of the judge's written notice that your appeal has been denied to file an additional (in this case, a third) appeal. This time, you have to file an appeal with the Social Security Administration Appeals Council. Again, you can get this form, known as the request for review of hearing decision/order, at your local Social Security office, or by calling the SSA's toll-free number, or off the SSA website.

As I said, the appeals council rarely reverses a judge's decision on a case that has already gone through the administrative law court. Often, the appeals council will find sufficient evidence to order a second administrative law hearing, at which point you will have to present your materials again, with special attention paid to one or another facet of your documentation that the appeals council has found significant. However, even if the chances that the appeals council will make a decision in your favor are slim, you must file an appeal with them before you are allowed to take your final and most drastic step, which is to file a lawsuit.

A lawsuit? You mean I can really take it that far?

People can and do take it that far, in large part because a negative decision from the SSA has a profound effect on their futures! Many people consider it important enough to go the full distance, despite the time, effort, and expense that it takes to mount a lawsuit. Most people consider the amount of money they would accumulate in the future if they were receiving full benefits for the rest of their lives, and they weigh this amount against what it costs to file a lawsuit. Usually, the amount of money and energy it takes to engage in the latter is less than the potential earnings that they stand to lose.

How much time do I have to file a lawsuit?

You must file the preliminary papers of a lawsuit against the Social Security Administration within 60 days of receiving written word of the SSA's denial of your appeal.

In the case of a lawsuit, is an attorney mandatory?

Absolutely. A lawyer who is conversant in Social Security law will be able to decide if a lawsuit is justified, and also to make a fairly good prediction as to whether you stand a chance of winning your case. If you decide to use a lawyer—and because your claim is for a significant amount, I would certainly advise retaining an attorney—you must notify the SSA of his or her appointment by filling out yet another form, this one known as the appointment of representative form.

How can I find an attorney who is familiar with Social Security law?

Look in the Yellow Pages of your phone book. If you know somebody who has been in a situation similar to yours, ask him for the name of the lawyer he or she used—there is nothing more valuable than a word-of-mouth recommendation. Most states have a council on aging or some other agency that is conversant with the problems of Social Security, age, and disabilities, and if they can't help you, chances are they will know who can. The SSA has stringent rules regarding lawyers—even your lawyers! Usually, they are allowed to charge you only if they win your appeal, and typically they will take one-quarter of the benefits that are past due (the benefits that are the subject of the dispute in the first place).

THE AMERICANS WITH
DISABILITIES ACT (ADA)

What exactly is the Americans with Disabilities Act?

The Americans with Disabilities Act, or ADA, was signed into law on July 26, 1990. The ADA is a federal law that was enacted to enable people with disabilities to enjoy the same civil rights that are enjoyed by people who do not suffer from disabilities. In short, this law says that consistent standards must be employed in both the private and the public sector, as well as in state and local government.

The ADA has five provisions, or parts, of which the first,

Equal Employment Opportunity, is perhaps the best known. Basically, this provision requires employers with a certain number of workers to provide "reasonable accommodation to qualified individuals with a disability." The second provision, Non-Discrimination on the Basis of Disability in State and Local Government Services, serves to provide access for the disabled to public transportation services. The third provision, Non-Discrimination on the Basis of Disability by Public Accommodations and Commercial Facilities, serves to provide access for the disabled to public places such as restaurants, hotels, and stores. The fourth provision, Telecommunications, serves to provide relay services for people who suffer from hearing impairments. The fifth and final provision, Miscellaneous Provisions, is a description of how the ADA affects other laws in existence.

What is the statutory meaning of a "qualified individual with a disability"?

Very briefly, a qualified individual with a disability is a person who meets legitimate skill, experience, education, and/or other requirements of an employment position of any kind. This individual must be able to perform the "essential functions" of the job in question with or without accommodation.

What is considered to be "reasonable accommodation"?

Basically, reasonable accommodation refers to any change or modification made to job requirements or the work environment that enables a qualified individual who is suffering from a disability to perform his or her work.

Does the ADA permit a potential employer to require a job applicant to take a medical examination before the employer makes a job offer?

No. An employer cannot require a job applicant to take a medical examination prior to making a job offer. But an employer can require that a post-offer medical examination prove that the applicant is able to perform all the necessary job-related tasks in a satisfactory manner.

Is a medical report from an evaluation performed by an employer considered to be part of an employee's general personnel record?
No. Employers are required to keep medical records confidential and separate from general personnel records.

Is it possible for an employer to be exempt from certain provisions of the ADA?
Yes. An employer can apply for an exemption, or modification, if that employer can prove that abiding by the law would cause him or her an undue hardship. According to the Equal Employment Opportunity Commission, the employer would have to demonstrate that accommodations made for the disabled would be "unduly costly, extensive, substantial, or disruptive, and would fundamentally alter the nature of the business."

Does the ADA grant a disabled individual any special attendance or leave-of-absence privileges?
No. Employers can require that all employees, regardless of disability, follow the set policies of the workplace.

Where can a worker file a formal ADA complaint?
Complaints can be filed with the Equal Employment Opportunity Commission (EEOC). You should also contact the EEOC for a complete list of all available ADA publications. Their contact information can be found in the Additional Resources section at the back of the book.

DEPENDENTS BENEFITS
FOR DISABLED WORKERS

What are dependents benefits?

Consider the difference between the amount of money that a disabled or retired worker needs to live alone—and how much money he or she may need if he or she has a spouse and/or children to support. Social Security offers dependents benefits to the children and/or the spouse of a disabled or retired worker, particularly if that worker's wages are the basis of what the family lives on.

Even if I don't literally "depend" on my spouse's salary, can I still be considered a dependent?

Yes.

I am a spouse of a disabled worker. Does this mean that I am automatically eligible for dependents benefits?

If you fall into one of the following categories, then you are eligible for dependents benefits:

- You are a spouse 62 years old, or older.
- You are a spouse under the age of 62 who is taking care of the disabled worker's child, who is either under the age of 16 or who was disabled before the age of 22.
- You are an unmarried child under age 18.
- You are an unmarried child, still in high school, and under age 19.
- You are an unmarried child of any age, disabled before the age of 22.

- You are an unmarried stepchild up to age 18, or, if you are still attending high school, age 19.
- You are a grandchild of the disabled worker and have been adopted by your grandparent, and your parents are unable to care for you, because they are either disabled or deceased.

SUPPLEMENTAL SECURITY INCOME (SSI)

I hear a lot about Supplemental Security Income. Can you explain it?

Supplemental Security Income, commonly known as SSI, is a state and federally operated program designed to ensure a minimum income to financially needy older and/or disabled Americans and to supplement their existing income, even if they are already receiving benefits from the Social Security Administration. Eligibility for the SSI program is based on your age, the extent of your disability, and your financial need. The last is determined based on your income and assets. Unlike regular Social Security benefits, SSI benefits are not related to your work history.

How do I know if I qualify for SSI benefits?

You will probably automatically qualify if your assets and your level of income are extremely low. The federal limit for a single person is $450 per month, $690 for a couple. People who are eligible for SSI are typically also eligible for Medicaid and food stamps, as well as a host of other free services provided by the state.

You are eligible for SSI benefits if:

You are a citizen of the United States, or a permanent legal resident, and

You are 65 or more years of age, and you are either blind or disabled, and

Your assets are worth less than $2,000, or $3,000, depending on whether you are single or married. Please note: The assets requirements are somewhat elastic, so even if your assets are worth more than the above figure, it is worth inquiring about you eligibility for SSI.

How does the SSA define "blind" and "disabled"?

Blind is defined by the SSA as having vision that is 20/200 or less with corrective lenses. The SSA considers a person to be disabled if he or she suffers from a mental or physical ailment that prevents him or her from doing normal work, and that doctors anticipate will last a year or more, or that will result in death.

If I am not a U.S. citizen am I eligible for SSI benefits?

No. As of August 1996, SSI benefits are normally available only to American citizens. This can be a very tough pill to swallow for older Americans who came legally to this country a long time ago but who never became U.S. citizens. If you are a noncitizen, you must meet one of the conditions below in order to be eligible for SSI:

- You are a legal resident of the U.S. who was already receiving SSI benefits on August 22, 1996
- You were a legal resident of the U.S. on August 22, 1996, and you are currently blind or disabled
- You are a legal resident of the U.S., you or your spouse have been employed for 10 or more years in this country, and during that time you or your spouse have

paid the minimum Social Security taxes in order to qualify for 40 quarters of work credits

- You are a legal resident of the U.S., and you or your spouse were honorably discharged from a branch of the U.S. military
- You were granted political asylum or refugee status by the Immigration and Naturalization Service. Bear in mind, however, that if you are in this situation, your SSI benefits will last only seven years after you come to the U.S.

Please note: The Social Security Administration provides disability benefits to qualified children under the SSI program. Generally, if a child has a condition that is associated with marked and severe functional limitations and is 18 years of age or younger, he or she is eligible for disability benefits. Another source of benefits for disabled children is the generosity of countless not-for-profit organizations that work to improve the quality of life for children living with a serious illness or injury. Disabled children stand to reap enormous benefits from these organizations, and though some organizations offer financial assistance, help does not always come in the form of a check. Many organizations offer support groups and medical equipment needed to care for seriously ill children. Educational, vocational, and recreational programs can help a disabled child to live as normal a life as possible.

I am a noncitizen who is not eligible for federal SSI benefits. Are any SSI benefits available to me?
If you are a noncitizen who was living in the United States as of August 22, 1996, and you are at least 65 years of age, then you may be eligible for SSI benefits, including food stamps, on

the state level. You may also be eligible for state SSI benefits if your immigration sponsor has died or become disabled. In this case, it is worth applying for both federal and state SSI benefits. If you are turned down on the federal level, you may find that you are eligible on the state level.

How does the SSA measure a person's income and assets?

The SSA does not calculate all income when it is assessing whether or not a person is eligible for its benefits. In fact, less than a half of a person's earned income is counted. In general, the federal SSI limits for income are approximately $450 a month, or about $5,400 annually. But just because your net income may be over the limit allowed by the SSA does not mean that you might not be eligible for state SSI benefits. By "income," the SSA means any money that you are bringing home as a result of employment; any money or income that you are receiving from investments or pensions; and any other benefits that you are receiving from another branch of Social Security, including survivors, dependents, retirement, or disability payments.

My wife and I receive free housing from her parents. Does the SSA figure in the value of our rent?

Yes. If you live with a friend or relative free of charge, the SSA will often reduce your monthly benefit. The rent you would be paying under normal circumstances is typically counted as income by the SSA.

Is any kind of income considered exempt from SSI calculations?

The SSA keeps a long list of the types of income it will not count as it determines your eligibility for SSI benefits. This list includes the first $65 of the wages that you receive from your employer every month, if applicable; 50 percent of your monthly earned income above that $65; any income from unpredictable or finite kinds of employment, such as a job that you perform only once or twice a month, provided this job does not earn you more than $100 monthly; any food stamps or housing or energy assistance you receive; and $20 per month that you receive from any source excluding regular Social Security benefits.

What about SSA regulations regarding the amount of assets I can own?

The general SSI ceiling on assets is about $2,000 for an individual and $3,000 combined for a married couple. The law may vary from state to state, so check the SSI regulations in the state where you live. But in general, when considering assets, the SSA will count any money or investments that you keep in your savings or checking account, and any real estate or furnishings that you possess.

I co-own a small piece of property with my brother. Does this count?

As far as the SSA is concerned, yes. The SSA will calculate how much it believes your share of that property is worth.

What assets are excluded from SSI calculations?

Some very, very critical ones! For example, your house and property, if you are living on that property at the time you apply for SSI benefits. The value of your car is also exempt from SSI asset calculations, up to a ceiling of $4,500. And if you use your car to travel to work (which most people do), or if you are disabled and your car is designed to accommodate that disability, then your car is not counted in SSI asset calculations at all.

Is any of my personal property exempt?

Yes, but only up to a ceiling of $2,000 ($3,000 for married couples). This includes your clothes, the furnishings of your house, and any appliances you may own.

How does the SSA calculate that $2,000? Based on what I originally paid for these items, or based on what they are worth now, used?

The SSA calculates that $2,000 maximum based on what those items would be worth in today's market.

What else is exempt from that $2,000 ceiling?

Your wedding and engagement rings. Even if they are worth $5,000 apiece, they are exempt. If you are disabled and need any special equipment to maintain that disability, including a hospital bed, or crutches, or a walker, or any special medical machines, these too are exempt.

My wife has a life insurance policy. Is that exempt?

If your wife's policy is worth $1,500 or less (per person), then it is exempt, as well. Remember, we are talking here about federal regulations. The state where you live may have different rules regarding income eligibility.

Is there any way to reduce my income or assets so that I may become eligible for SSI benefits?

Yes. If you are close to the levels of eligibility, but slightly over in terms of assets or income, the SSA will permit you to liquidate some of your holdings within a certain time period. If you apply for SSI benefits, and the agency deems your assets and income to be over federal limits for eligibility, the SSA will give you six months to liquidate your real estate holdings and three months to get rid of personal belongings and furnishings. But when the SSA says that you have to get rid of the property in question, they are not fooling around. You cannot simply transfer the title over to a friend or relative.

What is the typical SSI benefit amount for an individual and a couple?

Typically, the SSI provides benefits of approximately $500 a month for a single person, and approximately $750 a month for a married couple. Like every other benefits program offered by Social Security, these figures are adjusted on the first of every year for inflation.

Why isn't the SSI payment for an eligible couple twice that paid to an eligible individual?

The federal SSI program provides a very basic payment for an eligible individual and a larger amount for an eligible couple. The payment for a couple is lower than that made to two individuals because married people living together generally share expenses and are able to live more economically than two people living independently.

I have heard that some states will supplement what I receive from the federal SSI. Can you tell me what those states are?

These states are: California, Hawaii, Iowa, Michigan, Massachusetts, Maine, Nevada, Utah, Vermont, Wisconsin, New Jersey, New York, Rhode Island, Pennsylvania, and Washington, and the District of Columbia. In these states, your state supplement is automatically added to your federal supplement, so you only have to apply, and qualify, once, in order to receive both federal and state SSI benefits.

Should I assume that other states in the United States don't offer supplements?

No. Some states—Arkansas, Georgia, Texas, Tennessee, West Virginia, Mississippi, and Kansas—do not administer any supplements but the states listed below administer their own supplements and do not tie them to the federally administered SSI benefits. Consequently, you must apply to these programs separately. States that offer their own supplements are, in alphabetical order: Alabama, Alaska, Arizona, Colorado, Connecticut, Florida, Idaho, Illinois, Indiana, Kentucky, Louisiana, Maryland, Minnesota, Missouri, Nebraska, New Hampshire, New Mexico, North Carolina, North Dakota, Ohio, Oklahoma, Oregon, South Carolina, South Dakota, Virginia, and Wyoming.

Are there any limits to the amount of income I can earn while still receiving SSI benefits?

Yes. Remember, anything you earn over $65 a month is subject to penalty. For every $2 more than that $65 ceiling that you earn a month, your SSI benefits will be reduced by $1.

Is my eligibility for SSI benefits compromised in any way by the fact that I have children who, if worse came to worst, could help support me?

Your eligibility for SSI is not affected by your children's ability to help support you. However, any support they do give you is considered income for SSI purposes and could affect the amount of your payment.

I have been receiving SSI checks for several months, and my check has always arrived on the first of the month. I cash the check immediately to pay my rent, which is due on the first of the month as well. What happens when the first of the month falls on a Saturday? Must my rent be late because I can't cash my check until Monday?

If the first of the month falls on a Saturday, Sunday, or legal holiday, your SSI check should arrive on the previous banking day.

What should I do if my check does not arrive at the time it usually arrives?
Call your Social Security office immediately. Unfortunately, getting a replacement check sent out can take as long as three to four weeks. This is another reason why direct deposit can save you a lot of worry and hassle.

REPRESENTATIVE PAYEES

I have an elderly friend who receives SSI benefits. I'm concerned that she is unable to manage her money to pay her bills on time. Can Social Security help her?
Yes. When an individual who receives Social Security or SSI checks is unable to manage these benefits in his or her own best interest, the SSA will appoint a representative payee. The Social Security or SSI benefits are sent directly to the representative payee, who is responsible for using these funds to ensure the personal care and well-being of the beneficiary, and also for reporting any changes in the beneficiary's circumstances that could affect his or her eligibility. For more information on this service, call your local SSA office and ask about representative payees.

APPLYING FOR SSI BENEFITS

How do I apply for SSI benefits?
You can apply for federal SSI benefits at your local Social Security office. SSI is considered separate from other benefits, so

if you are applying for any other kind of benefits, your case-worker will not automatically assume that you also want to apply for SSI. If you live in a state that requires you to apply separately for state-administered SSI benefits, you will have to apply for those benefits at your local welfare department.

What sort of documentation will I need when I apply for SSI benefits?

You must bring with you the same kind of documentation that you would bring if you were applying for any kind of Social Security benefits, including your Social Security number. You must show the SSA office your birth certificate or your U.S. passport to prove that you are a U.S. citizen. And you must provide evidence of your assets and income so that the SSA can make a determination of your eligibility. If you own your own home (and remember that your house is exempt, provided you live there), you should bring either a copy of your most recent tax bill or any information associated with a mortgage. If you rent, the SSA requires a copy of your lease, as well as the name, address, and phone number of your landlord. You should also provide evidence of your paycheck, and all documentation relating to any assets you have, including the amount of money you have in your checking or savings accounts, or any other investments that you may own. If you do not have any of these documents, the SSA office can help you locate copies.

How often will the SSA check up on me to see whether I still qualify for SSI benefits?

At least once every three years. You will receive a notice of review in the mail, upon which you are obliged to produce the same kinds of documentation that you brought to the SSA office when you were originally applying for benefits, i.e., any updated information about your housing, your possessions, your investments, and your medical condition, if applicable. Generally, this SSI review can be done either via telephone or through the mail, though there are instances when you might have to make an appearance at your local SSA office.

How long will it take for my claim to be approved?

The review and determination process usually takes one or two months, at which point—assuming your application has been approved—you will be informed how much your benefits will be and when you can expect your first check.

What if I am desperate and I really need some money in a hurry?

If you are having a financial crisis, your Social Security office may provide you with some kind of interim payment while you wait for your application to be officially approved. Whatever monies you receive as this emergency payout will be deducted from your first SSI benefits check.

CIVIL SERVICE RETIREMENT BENEFITS

What are civil service retirement benefits?

An enormous number of Americans have been or are currently employed by agencies and departments of the federal government. These jobs often pay far less than comparable jobs in the private sector, but they do have one great advantage, and that is a very comprehensive retirement system. In fact, there are two federal retirement systems, the Civil Service Retirement System (CSRS) and the Federal Employees' Retirement System (FERS).

What is the difference between the Civil Service Retirement System and the Federal Employees' Retirement System?
Until 1984, every federal government worker in this country was part of the Civil Service Retirement System. These workers were not covered by the U.S. Social Security system. Starting January 1, 1984, any worker hired by the federal government was made a part of a different plan, called the Federal Employees' Retirement System. These workers *are* insured by Social Security.

What kinds of benefits are government employees hired before 1984 eligible for?
In 1984, employees hired before 1984 were given the option of remaining in their old system, the Civil Service Retirement System, or changing over to the Federal Employees' Retirement System. Both programs are administered by the U.S. government's Office of Personnel Management, known as the OPM, and both are funded by employees' payroll deductions, as well as by contributions from federal agencies. Both systems offer disability, retirement, and survivors benefits. But neither the CSRS nor the FERS offers dependents benefits. The rules regarding a worker's eligibility are different from the rules that the SSA uses for its policyholders. Also, the benefits are based on the worker's highest average salary for any three consecutive years of employment.

How do I know if I am eligible for either the CSRS or the FERS?

You are considered eligible if you have worked five or more years for the U.S. government as a civilian employee. This means that you can qualify for a government pension, also known as a retirement annuity. Also, if you have worked five or more years as a federal civilian employee, you are eligible to get retirement credit for any years after 1956 that you might have served in one or another branches of the military, provided you pay a premium based on the amount of your military pay.

Do these five years of employment have to be consecutive?
No, they do not.

What if I leave my federal government job and then return? Will my coverage pick up again?
If you worked in a federal government job prior to 1984, when the only retirement plan in existence for federal workers was the CSRS, and you left your place of employment, then came back to your place of employment after 1984, you may be entitled to benefits from both the CSRS and the FERS. Here are some variations on this theme:

If you worked in a government job for five or more years and left that government job prior to 1984, you are eligible to reenter the CSRS system if you commence a new job with the U.S. government after January 1, 1984. If for some reason you do not want to reenter the CSRS system, then you must enter the FERS system. If you accumulate at least five years of employment under the FERS system, too, then you may be eligible for retirement benefits under both the CSRS and the FERS systems.

If you left your government job for at least one year and you choose to reenter the CSRS system upon your return, you will also be covered by Social Security, as will FERS employees who leave their jobs for at least one year and then return. Bear in mind, though, that once you are eligible for both Social Security and CSRS retirement benefits, your CSRS benefits will be reduced by the amount of whatever Social Security benefits you receive as a direct result of your federal government employment. This is known as the pension offset rule, and it prevents most workers from receiving double the amount of retirement benefits.

Tell me about the retirement benefits offered by the CSRS and the FERS.

There are two kinds of retirement annuities offered under the CSRS and the FERS. One is an immediate annuity, and the other is a deferred annuity. An annuity is a type of investment in which you contract with an insurance company that invests on your behalf. (See *Ask Suze . . . About Mutual Funds and Annuities* for a more thorough discussion of annuities.)

What are my choices for taking my retirement benefits?

If you have worked for the federal government for five or more years, you are eligible to retire at age 62. At this point, you have a choice: you can immediately begin to receive an annuity paid out of your retirement account, to which you have been contributing through payroll deductions. Again, the five years that you worked for the federal government do not necessarily have to be consecutive, nor do you have to have served five years in the same department, i.e., you can switch agencies and still retain your retirement annuity. Or you may also take all of the money from your retirement account at once, if you so choose.

If you stop working for the federal government before you have reached the age of retirement, you cannot begin to draw your annuity immediately. You can leave the money that has accumulated in your CSRS or FERS system account in that account, or you can withdraw it in a lump sum. If you leave your money in the account, you are deferring your annuity payments until age 62—that's why it's called a deferred annuity. Or if you change your mind and decide that you want to withdraw your money before retirement, you can receive all of it in a lump sum anytime before you reach the age of 62.

Which of the options is preferable?

It will depend on how much of a monthly annuity income you are eligible for, compared to the income that your lump-sum withdrawal could generate if invested. If the monthly annuity sum equals 2 or 3 percent above what the going interest rate on a lump sum would generate, take the monthly annuity income. Otherwise, roll over the lump sum, invest the money on your own, and withdraw the income as needed.

My spouse has worked in a federal government job for 23 years. Is he entitled to any special benefits?

Because your spouse has worked at least 20 years in a federal government job, he is eligible to claim his immediate annuity at the slightly younger age of 60. This is just the tip of the iceberg as far as duration of service in federal employment is concerned. A worker who has served in a federal government job for 30 or more years and who is covered by the CSRS or the FERS is eligible to retire with a pension at age 55 (though beginning in the year 2002, this minimum retirement age will be rising at the rate of two months per year for both CSRS and FERS).

What happens if I am laid off from my federal government job before I become eligible for my pension?

The CSRS and the FERS both have rules in place that will permit some, though not all, long-term workers to take an immediate annuity even if they are laid off before retirement age. If the worker is covered under the CSRS and has been working for at least one year in the two years immediately preceding the date on which he or she was laid off, and is age 50 with 20 years of service, or any age with at least 25 years of service, that worker may be eligible to collect an immediate annuity.

One difference in eligibility requirements for a comparable worker covered by FERS is that he or she does not need to have been employed within the past two years before he or she was laid off. Another difference is that if the FERS employee claims his immediate annuity before he or she reaches age 55, the amount of that annuity is reduced by 2 percent for every year under the minimum retirement age of 55 the employee is.

My husband is an air-traffic controller. Are the rules for his job any different than they are for other government workers?

Yes. The federal government, noting the high-stress nature of such jobs as air-traffic controller and firefighter, as well as most law enforcement jobs, makes it easier for workers in these jobs to claim early retirement. The government also has lowered the minimum number of years that a worker in one of these fields has to serve in his or her job. If you are a police officer or a firefighter who is covered under CSRS, for example, you are permitted to claim your retirement benefits at age 50. If your husband the air-traffic controller is covered by the CSRS and he has been at his job for 20 years or longer, he can retire at age 50. If he has been working 25 years at his job, then he is eligible for his retirement benefits anytime he wants.

FEDERAL BENEFITS:
HOW MUCH AND HOW LITTLE

How do the CSRS and the FERS calculate how much my benefits will be?

Both systems use a variety of factors. The first is how long you have worked in your federal government job and how long you have been making contributions to the retirement fund. A second and equally important factor that both the CSRS and the FERS use to calculate the amount of your retirement annuity is what is known as a worker's high-three average salary.

What is a high-three average salary?

This represents worker's average salary over the three consecutive years in which the worker has received the highest amount of income. Let's say that in the three consecutive years your salary was highest, you earned $40,000, $40,000, and $42,000. These three annual salaries would be added up, for a grand total of $122,000, and then divided by three, for an average of approximately $40,666. Both the CSRS and the FERS base the retirement annuity that they will pay a worker on this high-three average salary, but the way each calculates the benefit is different.

How does the CSRS perform its calculations?

The CSRS starts with your high-three average salary. To that number, say $40,666, it adds 1.5 percent of your high-three average pay, times 5, for your first five years of service. Then it adds 1.75 percent of your high-three average pay, times the number of years more than five and less than ten you have been working at your job. Finally, it adds 2 percent of your high-three average pay, times the number of years more than ten that you have been working at your job. The grand total is the amount of your retirement annuity.

Do the CSRS and the FERS make any allowances for inflation?

Yes, just like the Social Security Administration, both systems make a yearly cost-of-living adjustment that is tied to the increases in the Consumer Price Index.

CSRS AND SOCIAL SECURITY

You mentioned earlier that anybody who is covered by the CSRS is generally not covered by Social Security. Are there any exceptions to this general rule?

It is fairly common for workers employed by the federal government to have had one or more jobs during their lifetime, including jobs that are insured by the Social Security Administration. If this is true for you, and you have built up enough work credits to qualify for Social Security benefits, then you can receive both your Social Security retirement benefits and your CSRS annuity.

What if I am receiving survivors benefits from Social Security? Can I still get my CSRS annuity?

Yes. If you are receiving either survivors or dependents benefits from Social Security based on your spouse's work history (as opposed to your own work record) and you are also eligible for a CSRS retirement annuity, you may receive both. However, your Social Security benefits may be drastically reduced, thanks to the pension offset rule.

By how much will my survivors benefits be reduced?
If you are receiving Social Security dependents benefits as well as a federal government annuity, your dependents benefits will be reduced by two-thirds the amount of your pension, which does not leave a whole lot.

FERS BENEFITS

How does the FERS calculate benefits?
The FERS calculates your retirement annuity by taking 1 percent of your high-three average and multiplying this number by the number of years you have spent in your job. You are also eligible to take early retirement under the FERS system (for a reduced benefit) if you have worked for 10 or more years at your federal government job.

By how much will my retirement annuity benefit be reduced if I take early retirement under the FERS system?
Your retirement annuity benefit will be reduced by 5 percent for each year under the age of 62 that you claim retirement.

That sounds like a lot to me. But are there any advantages to claiming early retirement, despite the big cut this will take out of my retirement annuity?
The base amount of your retirement annuity is going to be the same no matter whether you choose to exercise it at age 57, 59, or 61. This is because the FERS uses the high-three salary sys-

tem of calculation. And if you invest the money that you have taken out sensibly, the 5 percent per year may be offset.

I hear that the FERS offers something called an annuity supplement. What is this?

An annuity supplement is an additional sum of money given to longtime federal government employees. If you are 55 years old and you have been employed by the federal government for 30 or more years, or if you are 60 years old and you have been employed by the federal government for 20 or more years, you are eligible for this annuity supplement.

What happens if I take a job while I am receiving my annuity? Will I be penalized?

If you are under age 62 and you take on new employment after retiring from your federal government job, your *annuity supplement* will be reduced by $1 for every $2 you earn. I want to stress that it is your *supplement* that is affected, not your annuity.

Does the CSRS or the FERS offer any survivors benefits to spouses of deceased retirees?

Not necessarily. This is largely dependent on the choices that the federal worker makes upon his or her retirement. If the federal worker chooses to take a full retirement annuity, then no benefits at all will be paid to any of his survivors when he or she dies. However, this worker can choose to take an annuity with full survivors benefits, though if he or she does so, the amount of his or her own retirement annuity will be reduced. He or she can also choose to have survivors benefits paid to someone other than his or her current spouse. And there is a final option: The worker can elect a reduced survivors benefits package, which will reduce his own annuity, but not by as much as if he had chosen a full survivors benefits package.

Which of these packages makes the most sense?

The answer depends almost entirely on your situation. For example, if you are a federal government employee who is not married, has no dependents, and could use all the money that you have coming to you, it probably makes the most sense for you to accept the full retirement annuity without survivors benefits. Please note: If you are married and you choose this particular kind of retirement annuity, you and your spouse must fill out and have notarized a form that informs the Office of Personnel Management that your spouse has voluntarily waived the rights to survivors benefits.

If you are married at the time you become eligible for your retirement annuity, and you are willing to accept a little less in exchange for the comfort of knowing that your spouse will be taken care of after your death, go ahead and get the retirement annuity that offers full survivors benefits. If your current spouse is in agreement, you can even arrange for these survivors benefits to be paid to a former spouse!

Generally, you should keep several factors in mind when you are deciding what form your retirement annuity should take. If your spouse or beneficiary is much younger than you are, it makes sense for you to take a reduced retirement annuity, leaving the rest for a survivors benefit. That way, your spouse will have the advantage of receiving these benefits for a very long time. If you are a federal worker on the verge of retirement and you are much younger than your spouse, then I would look into taking full retirement benefits only if it was cost-effective and you have a whole-life insurance policy in place to protect your spouse in case you predecease him or her.

Otherwise, I would take out full survivors benefits to protect my spouse. Another question to ask yourself is how healthy you are and how many more years you believe you have left in your life (not that any of us can ever really predict this). You should also consider these questions when deciding if you should take out survivors benefits: Does your spouse or potential beneficiary have any income of his or her own? Does he or she really need the amount that a survivors benefit could provide? More than you do?

Tell me more about this variation on the retirement annuity that provides survivors benefits to someone who is not your spouse.

The CSRS and the FERS both offer a 55 percent survivors annuity that can be paid out to a person who is not the current spouse of the worker in question.

Will the amount of my own retirement annuity be affected by this survivor benefit?

Yes, but here is where the rules start to get a little complicated. If the person you name as your survivor beneficiary is either older than you or no more than five years younger than you, your own retirement annuity will be reduced by 10 percent. If your beneficiary is more than five years younger than you, your annuity will be reduced 5 percent for every additional five years. So, for example, your annuity will be reduced 15 percent if your beneficiary is between five and ten years younger; 20 percent if ten to fifteen years younger, and so on. If you are 60 and your beneficiary is 40, your retirement annuity will be reduced by 20 percent. If your beneficiary happens to die before you do, you can arrange to have your retirement annuity restored to what it would have been if you had not chosen a beneficiary. However, you cannot simply decide all of a sudden that naming a survivor beneficiary was a foolish move, and that you would like your retirement annuity to be restored to its normal amount.

What about a retirement annuity with reduced survivors benefits?

This is an option for a federal government worker who does not want his or her retirement annuity to be reduced as much as it would have been if he or she had chosen full survivors benefits but who still finds peace of mind in providing for his or her spouse in the event of his or her death. This particular facet of the FERS allows the retiring federal worker to divide up the pie, designating part of the amount in his or her retirement annuity to be used for his or her own retirement benefit and the rest to be set up to function as survivors benefits.

Is there a restriction on what percentage of this retirement annuity goes into which pile?

No, it is up to the worker.

When do survivors benefits terminate?

When the surviving spouse dies, or remarries before age 55.

DISABILITY BENEFITS FOR FEDERAL WORKERS

Do the CSRS and the FERS offer any benefits to employees who become disabled while they are working for the government?

Yes. If you have been employed by the federal government for at least five years, you are covered by the CSRS, and you become disabled before you reach retirement age, you may be eligible for disability benefits. If you are covered under the FERS, you need only have been employed by the federal government a year and a half, or 18 months, to be eligible for disability benefits.

How do the CSRS and the FERS define disability?

Both the CSRS and the FERS are far less specific in their definitions of "disabled" than the Social Security Administration. The CSRS and the FERS will deem a worker disabled if, quite simply, he or she is unable to perform his or her job because of disease or an injury of some kind. Both insurers are likely to question whether the worker can perform his or her job adequately, whether the agency or department where the federal employee works has made every conceivable effort to adapt, adjust, and modify the workplace to accommodate the needs of this disabled individual, and whether there is another comparable job within the same agency or department that could accommodate this injured or disabled worker.

What sort of evidence of disability do the CSRS and the FERS require? The same as the Social Security Administration, or are they more lenient in this department, too?

As was the case with Social Security disability eligibility, your physician must write a letter to the Office of Personnel Management describing your disability in detail. He or she must also note the date the disability started and explain why he or she believes that your particular disability prevents you from adequately performing your job. You can do your doctor and yourself a huge service if you describe to your doctor in detail exactly why and how your disability prevents you from carrying out your job in a satisfactory manner.

Your supervisor at your place of employment must also be involved in this decision. He or she must write a statement that describes your job and how he or she believes your disability will impair, or render impossible, your performance at work. He or she must also mention if there is a comparable position within the same department or agency that would be more appropriate for you given your disability. Again, your input could be extremely valuable.

Does my disability have to be a permanent one in order for me to receive disability benefits?

No, not necessarily. The federal government can require you to undergo an examination in order to assess whether your disability is temporary, or continuing, or permanent. Again, I would leave nothing to chance. Enlist the help of your doctor to draft a letter explaining the various ways in which your physical or mental ailment continues to prevent you from doing your job adequately. Ask your physician to send this letter directly to the government-appointed physician, so that the latter will have this letter on file.

How does the government define "recovered"?

The government officially considers a worker recovered if a thorough medical exam determines that he or she is no longer disabled, i.e., if he or she is able to resume performing his or her job. The government also considers a worker recovered if he or she is able to take a new job within the federal government, or if the worker is earning an annual income of 80 percent or more of his or her previous annual income, whether or not he or she is working for the federal government.

What if the government-appointed doctor considers my disability permanent?

If your disability is considered to be a continuing or permanent one, or if you reach the age of 60 without recovering from that disability, then you are eligible for permanent disability retirement benefits.

How much will my disability benefits come to?

The amount of your benefits depends on whether you are insured by the CSRS or the FERS. If you are insured by the CSRS, your benefits will be either 40 percent of your high-three average pay, or a percentage of the pension that you would have been eligible to receive had you continued working until age 60. Unfortunately, you will receive whichever of these two figures is lower. Let's say that your high-three average pay is $37,000. Forty percent of $37,000 is $14,800. Now let's look at the second calculation. The CSRS adds up the number of years you have worked at your job and the number of years that you have remaining until you reach age 60. Let's say that you have worked in your federal government job for 20 years, and at age 57, you have three years left before retirement. The bean-counters at the CSRS take this figure, 23, and multiply your high-three salary average by a corresponding percentage that relates to the number of years you've worked. You are eligible to receive the lower of these two figures.

Here's an example to show you how this works. Let's say you are 57 years old, you've worked for 18 years on the job, and you've decided to take your pension early. You are faced with one of two possible benefit amounts: You will either receive 40 percent of your high-three average pay, or a portion of the pension you would have received had you kept on working until age 60.

Let's say that your high-three average pay was $40,000. Forty percent of that would be $16,000. That's one amount. As for the other amount, add together your total years of service—18—plus the number of years remaining until you reach age 60—three years. This gives us a total of 21. Now the CSRS number-crunchers multiply your high-three average salary by approximately 36 percent (for 20 to 22 years of service) to arrive at the figure of $14,400 (36 percent multiplied by 23). Unfortunately, you are obliged to accept the lower of the two payments, which in this case is $14,400.

If you are insured by the FERS, your disability payments are variable and depend on a number of factors. During the first year of your disability, you will receive approximately 60 percent of your high-three average pay, minus any Social Security benefits that you may be receiving concurrently. During the second year, this percentage drops to 40 percent again, minus any Social Security benefits that you may be receiving concurrently. When you reach age 62, the FERS bean-counters begin calculating what your retirement annuity would have come to if you had worked without interruption until age 62. How do they reach the final figure that you will be paid for the duration of your life? They count your total years of employment by the federal government and add to this the number of years (up to age 62) you have been receiving disability. Then they multiply this figure by your high-three average income and add to the final figure whatever increases for inflation have been considered since you went on disability.

Is there a cost-of-living adjustment with FERS disability benefits payouts?

Yes, though unlike the adjustments we have seen so far, the FERS formula takes the cost-of-living index and subtracts a single percentage point from it.

CSRS AND FERS
SURVIVORS BENEFITS

Do the CSRS and the FERS provide any benefits to the surviving spouse or family of a deceased government worker?
Yes.

How do I know if I am eligible for survivors benefits?
If you are the surviving spouse or child of a federal government worker who was employed by the federal government for at least 18 months and who died while working for the government, you are eligible to receive survivors benefits.

Did my deceased spouse and I have to have been married a certain length of time in order for me to collect survivors benefits?
You and your deceased spouse had to have been married for at least a year at the time of his or her death.

Do I have to be a certain age before I can collect survivors benefits?
No.

My husband and I were both employed by the federal government. Last year he had a heart attack at work and died. Am I eligible for survivors benefits, even though I am also an employee in the same system?
Yes. In fact, you are eligible to collect both your own retirement benefits and the benefits that you have coming to you as

a surviving spouse (provided you and your deceased husband had been married for longer than a year at the time of his death).

What about my children? Are they eligible for survivors benefits as well?

Yes, each child is eligible for survivors benefits until he or she reaches age 18 or gets married, whichever comes first.

Are there any exceptions for students?

Yes. If a child is a full-time student in high school or college, then his or her survivors benefits will continue until he or she reaches age 22.

My boyfriend was a federal government worker who died in the workplace last year. Although we were never married, we do have a son. Is my son eligible for any survivors benefits?

Yes, your son does qualify for survivors benefits, provided the deceased worker recognized and established his paternity.

Do stepchildren qualify for survivors benefits?

If the stepchild lived with the deceased worker and enjoyed a traditional parent-child relationship with him or her (was clothed, sheltered, supported by the stepparent), the answer is yes.

CSRS SURVIVORS BENEFITS: HOW MUCH?

How much will the surviving spouse of a deceased federal government worker receive if the deceased worker was insured by the CSRS?

If you are the surviving spouse of a worker who died while employed by the federal government, you are eligible to receive an annuity. For a spouse, the amount of the annuity comes to approximately 55 percent of the retirement annuity that the deceased worker accumulated before his or her death.

What if I remarry? Will I lose my survivors annuity?

It depends on when you remarry. If you remarry before you reach age 55, you will lose your annuity. If you remarry after the age of 55, your annuity will continue unabated.

What if I remarry before I am 55 and my second marriage ends? Can I become eligible for my first husband's annuity again?

Yes, you may arrange to have your survivors annuity reinstated.

What about survivors benefits for my 13-year-old son?

The amount of a survivors annuity for a child of a deceased government employee who was insured under the CSRS depends on whether or not the child has a living parent. If there is a surviving parent, the child is eligible to receive approximately 60 percent of the deceased worker's high-three average pay, divided by the number of children who are claiming benefits.

What if my son is left with no surviving parents?

In this situation, the child receives an annuity based on approximately 75 percent of the high-three average pay of the deceased worker, divided by the number of eligible children.

FERS SURVIVORS BENEFITS

How are FERS survivors benefits different from CSRS survivors benefits?

As far as survivors benefits to a child are concerned, FERS benefits differ from CSRS benefits in one important respect: If the child in question is also receiving Social Security dependents benefits, his FERS survivors benefits will be reduced. If you are the surviving spouse of a FERS-insured federal government worker, the amount of your benefits will be determined by the number of years that the deceased worker was employed by the government. If the deceased worker was employed by the federal government for more than 18 months but for fewer than 10 years, then the surviving spouse typically receives a single lump-sum payment (adjusted every year for inflation) of roughly $21,000 to $22,000. If the deceased worked at his or her government job for longer than 10 years, the surviving spouse is eligible to receive an annuity equal to approximately half of what the deceased worker's retirement annuity would have been if he had continued working.

Is this survivors annuity reduced in any way by Social Security benefits payments?
No.

I am the surviving spouse of a FERS-insured worker who died on the job. How do I go about applying for survivors benefits?
You must submit an application to the Office of Personnel Management. (See Additional Resources for contact information.)

VETERANS' BENEFITS

My husband is a veteran. Does he receive any special consideration from the SSA?
Yes, but it takes the form of extra work credits rather than more money. If your husband served in active duty between

September 1, 1940, and December 31, 1956, he is eligible for an earnings credit equivalent to an additional $160 a month. If he served in active duty from 1957 to 1977, he will receive an extra $300 worth of earnings credits per quarter, and if he served in active duty anytime after 1977, he will receive $100 worth of earnings credit for every $300 of military pay he received during that period, up to an annual maximum of $1,200.

Who is eligible for veterans' benefits?

Veterans Administration (VA) benefits are available to women and men who were engaged in active service in one or another of the uniformed branches of the U.S. military. This includes the Army, the Navy, the Air Force, the Marines, the Coast Guard, the WAAC (Women's Army Auxiliary Corps), and the WASP (Women's Air Service Pilots). VA benefits include disability compensation and training, education, home loans, insurance services, burial benefits, healthcare services, and vocational rehabilitation, among others. For a complete listing of VA services and benefits, access their website at *www.va.gov*.

What about the National Guard?

Generally, no, unless the National Guard has been called up for active duty. This situation is known as active duty for training, and is considered the same as active duty.

What is the exact definition of the term "active duty"?

Active duty simply means full-time—as opposed to part-time—service in one of the organizations mentioned above.

Does the active duty have to have been for any particular length of time?

No. The only exception is with pensions for indigent disabled veterans. Eligibility requires at lest 90 days of active service.

VETERANS' DISABILITY

Tell me about disability benefits for veterans. Who is eligible?

If you are a veteran suffering from a disability that occurred while you were in active duty in the military service, you are eligible for benefits. Your disability or injury or aggravation of a past injury has to have occurred while you were serving on active duty, or on active duty for training.

What if I was disabled during peacetime?

The VA is relatively lenient about this, especially since much of active duty is actually daily responsibilities and preparation. Even if you sustained your injury while you were on leave during a time of war, the VA will still allow you to be compensated for your injury.

What does the VA consider a time of war?

World War I; World War II; the Korean War; the Vietnam War; and the Persian Gulf War.

How much are the typical benefits offered to a disabled serviceman or servicewoman?

The amounts vary, ranging from $100 a month, or $1,200 a year, for a slight disability, to around $2,000 a month, or $24,000 a year, for a major disability. Your disability is given a rating by VA doctors and other military personnel, and you are given a percentage that is supposed to represent the extent to which your disability interferes with your ability to earn a living.

What if my disability does not show up for a long time? Or what happens if it worsens over time?

This was certainly the tragic case with Agent Orange, the chemical that many Vietnam veterans were exposed to during their tours of active duty. The symptoms of exposure to this chemical did not show up until much later, and many veterans groups had an extremely difficult time convincing the VA that the symptoms and the conditions they were suffering were connected with their tours of active duty.

In answer to your question, you can claim disability benefits even if the symptom or the disease does not show up immediately. If your injury or disability worsens over time, you can apply for an upgrade of your condition, which will increase the benefits that you have coming to you every month.

Are any benefits available to veterans with disabilities that are not the result of their time in the service?

Yes. Indigent veterans whose disabilities do not result from military service may receive a pension. To be eligible for this benefit, a veteran has to have served at least 90 days of active duty, and one of those days has to have occurred during one of the periods of war mentioned above. If the veteran meets these requirements, the small pension that he or she receives will simply bring up the amount of any benefits that he or she is already receiving, from Social Security or SSI, for example, to the congressionally mandated subsistence level, i.e., $9,000 annually.

Does the VA provide survivors benefits to the spouses of men and women who have served in active duty?

Yes. You must have been married to the veteran in question for at least one year and have been married to that person when he or she died. Unlike regular Social Security survivors benefits, VA survivors benefits can't be claimed if you were divorced or separated from the veteran when he died. If you remarry following the death of the veteran, you also are prohibited from claiming survivors benefits. However, if that second marriage ended for whatever reason—divorce or death—then you again are eligible for survivors benefits based on the marriage to the veteran.

What is the DIC benefit?

DIC stands for the dependency and indemnity compensation benefit. This benefit is given to the surviving spouse of a serviceman or servicewoman who died while engaged in active duty or as a result of a service-connected disability after he or she was discharged from the armed forces.

Is the spouse of a veteran who was dishonorably discharged eligible for the DIC benefit?

No.

How does the VA calculate out how much the DIC benefit will be?

The VA makes its financial determination based on the most advanced rank held by the veteran in question. The surviving spouses of the highest-ranking officers receive from $1,500 to $1,800 dollars per month, while the surviving spouses of the lowest-ranking members of the military generally receive roughly a third of that amount, or $500 to $600, per month.

If I have sizable assets or a full-time job will my DIC benefit be reduced?

No.

What is the aid & attendance benefit?

The A&A benefit is an additional sum of money that the VA gives to the surviving spouse of a serviceman or servicewoman who died while serving on active duty if that spouse lives in a nursing home or is confined to his or her house. The amount of this benefit is determined in part by the amount of assets owned by the surviving spouse and by the amount of medial expenses that the surviving spouse has.

Because my husband is a veteran, is he automatically eligible for medical care at a Veterans Administration hospital?

If you are a veteran with a service-connected disability, or a veteran's dependent or survivor, and you are unable to afford medical care at a traditional hospital, then you are eligible for full care at one of the many VA hospitals across the United States. The only downside to VA hospitals is that they are often fully occupied, so you may not be able to get the care you need when you need it. For this reason, the VA has set out a triage system for people needing care, with veterans in emergency getting first priority, and survivors and dependents who need care and can't afford it elsewhere coming in last.

How can I find out more about the programs the Veterans Administration offers veterans and their dependents?

The VA operates hundreds of offices around the country, both in cities and in small towns. Look in the Yellow Pages under U.S. Government. Or you can access the Veterans Administration website at *www.va.gov.*

· · ·

There you have it, Social Security "in a nutshell." I know how complicated Social Security policy can be—made even worse by the fact that the regulations tend to change every few years. But you've made it through and, I suspect, you will find yourself consulting various parts of this book time and again as you and those you love grow older.

It's also important to be aware of Social Security as a changing entity, for it will have to change radically in the coming generations, or it will cease to exist. As we discussed in these pages, extensive changes will have to be made to this system, which, like the population it was meant to protect, is aging and in increasing need of attention. As the baby boomers reach retirement age, Social Security will become an issue at the forefront of American debate. It's so very important that we leave our children and their children a legacy of protection and not debt. In the 21st century, our children deserve to be sustained by a thriving and resourceful governmental agency that was surely one of the 20th century's most humane and civilized inventions.

Additional Resources

National Organizations

American Association of Retired Persons (AARP)
601 E Street, NW
Washington, DC 20049
(800) 424-3410

American Bar Association
Commission on Legal Problems of the Elderly
740 15th Street, NW
Washington, DC 20005-1022
(202) 662-8690
www.abanet.org

The American Council of the Blind
1115 15th Street NW, Suite 1004
Washington, DC 20005
(202) 467-5081 or (800) 424-8666
www.acb.org

American Foundation for the Blind
11 Penn Plaza, Suite 300
New York, NY 10001
(212) 502-7600 or (800) 232-5463

Braille Institute of America, Inc.
741 North Vermont Avenue
Los Angeles, CA 90029
(213) 663-1111

The Council for Disability Rights
205 West Randolph, Suite 1650
Chicago, IL 60606
(312) 444-9484
www.disabilityrights.org

National Council on Aging
409 3rd Street, SW, Suite 200
Washington, DC 20024
(202) 479-1200

National Council of Senior Citizens
8403 Colesville Road, Suite 1200
Silver Spring, MD 20910-3314
(301) 578-8800

New Eyes for the Needy
P.O. Box 332
549 Milburn Avenue
Short Hills, NJ 07078
(973) 376-4903

Family Caregiver Alliance
690 Market Street, Suite 600
San Francisco, CA 94104

(415) 434-3388
www.caregiver.org
Serving the families of people with Alzheimer's disease and other
neurological conditions

National Legal Aid and Defender Association
1625 K Street NW, Suite 800
Washington, DC 20006
(202) 452-0620
www.nlada.org

National Parent to Parent Support and Information System, Inc.
P.O. Box 907
Blue Ridge, GA 30513
(706) 374-3822
Devoted to linking parents of children with special health-care
needs and rare disorders

GOVERNMENT
AGENCIES

Administration on Aging
330 Independence Avenue, SW
Washington, DC 20201
(202) 619-0724

National Aging Information Center
330 Independence Avenue, SW, Room 4656
Washington, DC 20201
(202) 401-4634

National Institute on Aging
P.O. Box 8057
Gaithersburg, MD 20890-8057
(301) 496-1752

Social Security Administration
6401 Security Boulevard
Baltimore, MD 21235
(800) 234-5772
www.ssa.gov

Equal Employment Opportunity Commission
1801 L Street NW
Washington, DC 20507
(800) 669-4000
(800) 669-6820 (TTY)
www.eeoc.gov

Department of Veterans Affairs
245 West Houston Street
New York, NY 10014
(800) 827-1000

Internal Revenue Service
For "The Older Americans' Tax Guide," also known as Publication
544, and/or IRS Publication 915, which provides you with a number of worksheets to use to calculate the exact taxation of your benefits, call the IRS toll-free at (800) 829-3676.

Or go to *www.irs.ustreas.gov* and download these publications.

STATE OFFICES

ALABAMA
Commission on Aging
770 Washington Avenue, Suite 470
Montgomery, AL 36130
(334) 242-5743
Fax: (334) 242-5594

ALASKA
Commission on Aging
Department of Administration
Juneau, AK 99811-0209
(907) 465-3250

ARIZONA
Aging and Community Services Division
Economic Security Department
1789 West Jefferson Street, #950 A
Phoenix, AZ 85005
(602) 542-4446

ARKANSAS
Aging and Adult Services
P.O. Box 1437, Slot 1412
Little Rock, AR 72201
(501) 682-2441

CALIFORNIA
Department of Aging
1600 K Street, 4th floor
Sacramento, CA 95814
(916) 322-3887

COLORADO
Aging and Adult Services Division
110 16th Street, Suite 200
Denver, CO 80202
(303) 620-4147

CONNECTICUT
Elderly Services Division
25 Sigourney Street, 10th floor
Hartford, CT 06106-5033
(860) 424-5277

DELAWARE
Aging Division
1901 North Dupont Highway
New Castle, DE 19720
(302) 577-4791

DISTRICT OF COLUMBIA
Aging Office
441 4th Street, NW, Suite 900
Washington, DC 20001
(202) 724-5622

FLORIDA
Department of Elder Affairs
Building B, Suite 152
4040 Esplanade Way
Tallahassee, FL 32399-7000
(904) 414-2000

GEORGIA
Aging Services Office
2 Peachtree Street, NE, 18th floor
Atlanta, GA 30303
(404) 657-5258

GUAM
Division of Senior Citizens
Dept. of Public Health and Social Services
P.O. Box 2816
Agana, Guam 96932
(011) (671) 475-0263

HAWAII
Hawaii Executive Office on Aging
250 S. Hotel Street #107
Honolulu, HI 96813
(808) 586-0100

IDAHO
Idaho Commission on Aging
3380 Americana Terrace, #120
Boise, ID 83706
(208) 334-3833

ILLINOIS
Department on Aging
421 East Capital Avenue, Suite 100
Springfield, IL 62701-1789
(217) 785-3356

INDIANA
Disability, Aging, and Rehabilitative Services Division
Family and Social Services
402 West Washington Street, Room W454
P.O. Box 7083
Indianapolis, IN 46204
(317) 232-7000

IOWA
Elder Affairs Department
Clemens Building, 3rd floor
200 10th Street
Des Moines, IA 50309-3609
(515) 281-5187

KANSAS
Department on Aging
New England Building
503 South Kansas Avenue
Topeka, KS 66603-3404
(785) 296-4986

KENTUCKY
Aging Services Division
Social Services Department
275 East Main Street, 6 West
Frankfurt, KY 40621
(502) 564-6930

LOUISIANA
Elderly Affairs Office
P.O. Box 80374
412 North 4th Street, 3F
Baton Rouge, LA 70802
(504) 342-7100

MAINE
Bureau of Elder and Adult Services
35 Anthony Avenue
State House, Station 11
Augusta, ME 04333
(800) 262-2232 and (207) 624-5335

MARYLAND
Aging Office
State Office Building, Room 1007
301 West Preston Street
Baltimore, MD 21201-2374
(410) 767-1100

MASSACHUSETTS
Executive Office of Elder Affairs
1 Ashburton Place, 5th floor
Boston, MA 02108
(617) 727-7750

MICHIGAN
Aging Office
P.O. Box 30026
Lansing, MI 48909-8176
(517) 373-8230

MINNESOTA
Minnesota Board on Aging
444 Lafayette Road
St. Paul, MN 55155
(612) 296-2770

MISSISSIPPI
Aging and Adult Services Division
750 State Street
Jackson, MS 39202
(601) 359-4925

MISSOURI
Aging Division
Social Services Department
P.O. Box 1337
615 Howerton Court
Jefferson City, MO 65109
(573) 751-3083

MONTANA
Senior and Long-term Care Division
Department of Public Health and Human Services
P.O. Box 4210
111 Sanders, Room 211
Helena, MT 59604
(406) 444-7788

NEBRASKA
Department of Health and Human Services
Division on Aging
P.O. Box 95044
301 Centennial Mall South
Lincoln, NE 68509
(402) 471-2307

NEVADA
Aging Services Division
Human Resources Department
State Mail Room Complex
340 N. 11th Street, #203
Las Vegas, NV 89101
(702) 486-3545

NEW HAMPSHIRE
Elderly and Adult Services Division
115 Pleasant Street
Annex Building 1
Concord, NH 03301-3843
(603) 271-4680

NEW JERSEY
Department of Health and Senior Services
Division of Senior Affairs
P.O. Box 807
Trenton, NJ 08625-0807
(609) 292-7837

NEW MEXICO
State Agency on Aging
La Villa Rivera Building, 4th floor
224 East Palace Avenue
Santa Fe, NM 87501
(505) 827-7640

NEW YORK
Aging Office
Empire State Plaza, Building 2
Albany, NY 12223-1251
(800) 342-9871

NORTH CAROLINA
Resources for Seniors
1001 Navaho Drive
Raleigh, NC 27609
(919) 872-7933

NORTH DAKOTA
Aging Services
600 South 2nd Street, #1C
Bismarck, ND 58540
(701) 328-8910

OHIO
Aging Department
50 West Broad Street, 9th floor
Columbus, OH 43215-5928
(614) 466-5500

OKLAHOMA
Aging Services
P.O. Box 25352
312 NE 28th Street
Oklahoma City, OK 73125
(405) 521-2327 or (405) 521-2281

OREGON
Senior and Disabled Services Division
500 Summer Street, NE
Salem, OR 97310-1015
(503) 945-5811

PENNSYLVANIA
Department of Aging
555 Walnut Street, 5th floor
Harrisburg, PA 17101-1919
(717) 783-1550

PUERTO RICO
Office of Elderly Services
50063 Old San Juan Station
San Juan, Puerto Rico 00902
(787) 721-5710

RHODE ISLAND
Elderly Affairs Department
160 Pine Street
Providence, RI 02903
(401) 277-2858

SOUTH CAROLINA
Office on Aging
P.O. Box 8206
Columbia, SC 29211-8206
(803) 253-6177

SOUTH DAKOTA
Adult Services and Aging Office
Kneip Building
700 Governors Drive
Pierre, SD 57501-2291
(605) 773-3656

TENNESSEE
Aging Commission
500 Deaderic Street, 9th floor
Nashville, TN 37243-0860
(615) 741-2056

TEXAS
Aging Department
4900 North Lamar, 4th floor
Austin, TX 78751
(512) 424-6840

UTAH
Aging and Adult Services
120 North 200 West
P.O. Box 45500
Salt Lake City, UT 84145-0500
(801) 538-3910

VERMONT
Aging and Disability Department
103 South Main Street
State Complex
Waterbury, VT 05676
(802) 241-2400

VIRGINIA
Aging Department
1600 Forest Avenue, #102
Richmond, VA 23219-2327
(804) 662-9333

WASHINGTON
Adult and Aging Services
P.O. Box 45050
Olympia, WA 98504-5050
(360) 586-8753

WEST VIRGINIA
West Virginia Bureau of Senior Services
Holly Grove Building
1900 Kanawha Boulevard
Charleston, WV 25305-0160
(304) 558-3317

WISCONSIN
Aging and Long Term Care Bureau
P.O. Box 7851
Madison, WI 53707
(608) 266-2536

WYOMING
Aging Division
117 Hathaway Building, Room 139
Cheyenne, WY 82002-0710
(307) 777-7986

For information about Social Security application forms and/or benefits packages, you should contact the U.S. Office of Personnel Management's Retirement Information Office at (202) 606-0400. If you are calling for answers to questions that do not directly involve your or your spouse's employment history, you should call (202) 606-0500.

You may write to:
The U.S. Office of Personnel Management
Employee Services and Records Center
Boyers, PA 16017

INDEX

ABOUT THE AUTHOR

Suze Orman is the author of the #1 *New York Times* bestsellers *The 9 Steps to Financial Freedom* and *The Courage to Be Rich* and the national bestseller *You've Earned It, Don't Lose It.* A Certified Financial Planner® professional, she directed the Suze Orman Financial Group from 1987 to 1997, served as Vice President of Investments for Prudential Bache Securities from 1983 to 1987, and from 1980 to 1983 was an account executive at Merrill Lynch. She has hosted two PBS specials, one based on *The 9 Steps to Financial Freedom* and the other on *The Courage to Be Rich,* and is currently a financial contributor to NBC News' *Today.* She lectures widely throughout the United States and has appeared on *Dateline,* CNN, and CNBC, and has made numerous appearances on *The Oprah Winfrey Show.*